Rules of Engagement:
Mending Citizen/Police Interactions

B.L. Brown

Copyright © 2017 B.L. Brown

All rights reserved.

DEDICATION

This book is dedicated to officers and community members who are committed to building bridges between law enforcement and the communities they serve.

Thank you Kenny for your friendship, feedback and support.

Thank you Bronda and Val for your unconditional friendship and support.

A special thank you to Jae for your time, hard work, love and unwavering support. You are appreciated more than you will ever know!

CONTENTS

I.	CRIME DEFINED	4
II.	THE POLICE	28
III.	COMMUNICATING	54
IV.	POLICE/CITIZEN ENCOUNTERS	81
V.	POLICE TRAINING	108
VI.	SEARCH & SEIZURE	132
VII.	VEHICULAR ENCOUNTERS	146
VIII.	OTHER NOTEABLE OFFENSES	178
IX.	FAMILY VIOLENCE	188
X.	AFTER AN ARREST	198
XI.	CHILDREN	209
XII.	CREATING CHANGE	223
	EPILOGUE	233

The job of a police officer is a dangerous one, but one that I have found to be very rewarding. My experiences in law enforcement began when I was a child, dreaming of myself walking a patrol beat in my neighborhood. I was not sure why I was having this dream until the day I decided to abandon my patrol vehicle at a corner and walk through my assigned patrol area. This was not some suburban neighborhood that I was assigned to, but a neighborhood that included one of the most dangerous housing projects in the city. That walk gave many community members the courage to come outside their homes and enjoy the fresh air because they knew the police were there. I took the opportunity to go onto people's porches and converse with them about all sorts of things. It was at that moment on that day that I remembered the dream and discovered it was not **my** neighborhood that I was proudly patrolling but the one that I had adopted as my own, my assigned patrol zone. If there is to be change in the relationship between officers and the communities we are charged with protecting it will require our officers to not just take ownership of the areas they patrol but to positively engage with people within those communities. At the same time it is imperative that citizens take ownership of their communities and positively engage with officers. Rules of Engagement: Mending Citizen/Police Interactions can help citizens understand how to positively engage with officers. Together, WE can be the change!

B.L. Brown

DISCLAIMER

THE OPINIONS EXPRESSED IN THIS BOOK ARE NOT THE OPINIONS OF CURRENT OR PREVIOUS EMPLOYERS.

ALSO THE EXAMPLES, NAMES, STATISTICS AND CITIES USED ARE PURELY FICTIOUS AND ARE IN NO WAY RELATED TO ANY REAL PERSONS, PLACES, EVENTS OR SITUATIONS.

THIS BOOK SHOULD NOT BE USED AS LEGAL ADVICE.

This book is not to be used as legal advice, but should provide insight into the criminal justice system; how it operates, and how its operation impacts the average citizen.

GLOSSARY

Although a glossary of terms is common in some books, I felt that placing these definitions in the beginning of the book would help the reader to understand some concepts discussed on the following pages.

Arrest is when a person's liberty to come and go as they please is restrained, no matter how slight such restraint may be, according to Georgia Supreme Court.

Articulable Reasonable Suspicion is when there is enough information to cause a *reasonable law enforcement* officer (taking into account his or her knowledge, training, and experience) to reasonably believe that the person who is going to be detained is, was, or is about to be involved in criminal activity. The officer must be able to express that their belief is more than a hunch. This standard is less than probable cause, so it cannot be used to make an arrest, but can be used only for a brief detention.

Child is defined as, according to Georgia House Bill 242, a person under the age of 17 when they are accused of committing a criminal offense, a child is also defined as a person under the age of 21 years who committed a criminal offense before they reached 17 years of age and was under court supervision or probation.

Field Investigation- When patrol officers conduct investigations, while on patrol they are called field investigations. An example is when an officer stops someone and asks questions to investigate a complaint or observation of suspected unlawful behavior.

Justice is administering what is just by law and the administering of a deserved punishment or reward.

Probable cause is when a reasonable *person* believes a crime has been or is being committed. This requires only a probability, less than being certain, that a crime has been or is being committed, but more than just having a mere suspicion or hunch that a crime has been or is being committed.

Rank Structure- The police department's rank structure can vary. In some agencies the rank structure may be officer, sergeant, lieutenant, captain, major, deputy chief, and chief. In others, there may be a corporal between the officer and the sergeant. In some agencies, detective may be a rank rather than just a position, and in some agencies, there may be no deputy chief, only a chief. Any of these combinations could exist. It all depends on the agency.

Uniform Crime Reporting (UCR) is used by governments, media and students to research crime statistics nationally. Because these statistics are compiled in a uniform format, it makes them easy to compare and track. The uniform format means each crime has a specific definition that is consistent throughout the country. The FBI receives, compiles and stores these statistics.

1
CRIME: How It Is Defined

Rule 1: *Knowing how crime is defined by politicians, law enforcement agencies and citizens can help us understand how and why police departments deploy assets.*

News outlets talk about crime all the time. We hear mayors, commissioners, and police chiefs talk about crime and provide us with all of these official terms and statistics. Citizens who watch the news see and hear of people being shot, homes being burglarized and cars being rummaged through in their neighborhoods. The media can provide a perception that crime is more prevalent than it is in some neighborhoods and likewise can give the perception that crime is not as prevalent in other neighborhoods. This is accomplished by reporting about crime in some areas but failing to report crime in other areas giving the public the perception that crime is high in the reported area and low in the non-reported areas.

Politicians can also influence how citizens perceive crime by quoting crime statistics. Politicians in local areas do not want their citizens to be alarmed by media reports of crime in their neighborhood, so they turn to uniform statistics to provide the perception that all is well and it really isn't as bad as the media frames it. For example, when people complain about the number of shootings that have been reported on the news, a politician may indicate "violent crimes are down 10%". This statistic could be a comparison with the previous year, or it could be a comparison of any year that the percentage of violent crime was highest.

Statistics can be presented to provide any picture someone wants you to see. If the goal is to make citizens feel safe, the statistics will paint that picture. Various groups of people have a multitude of agendas when it comes to crime statistics. The police want you to feel safe thus they will report statistics that indicate crime is not excessively high. Real estate developers also want there to be a perception of a low crime rate. Those developers and real estate agents are in the business to sell property. People typically do not purchase in areas that do not appear to be safe.

> TIP: Based on my experience as a real estate agent and police officer, I suggest if you are looking to purchase a home, check with the local police department to determine what the crime rates are in the prospective neighborhood. Specific questions to ask, include how many burglaries have occurred in the area, what are the crime trends in the area (meaning what types of crimes occur in the neighborhood & when do they occur) and have there been any violent crimes in the area. You should also visit the area on weekend days, weekend nights, week days and week nights to see exactly how people behave in the neighborhood. Signs of a good neighborhood include well-manicured lawns.

On the other hand, a motivation for real estate developers and politicians to present current community members with high crime rates would be to encourage those residents to move abruptly. In some instances this causes property prices to fall, thus allowing those developers to purchase property at lower rates, increasing the potential for higher profits. Real estate investors who participate in providing low-income housing have a vested interest in high crime rates. Potential homeowners view neighborhoods with high crime rates as undesirable, resulting in lower cost properties.

The undesirable properties are then rented to low-income tenants through government programs. These programs often guarantee a certain price for a specific number of bedrooms and bathrooms in a home. Often these homes are not in subdivisions that have active homeowner associations; thus there is no pressure applied to these homeowners to maintain their property or complete improvements to their property in a timely manner. Crime rates can be skewed to paint whatever picture the presenter wants to get across to their audience.

Webster defines "crime" in the following manner:

"Crime is an action or an instance of negligence that is deemed injurious to the public welfare or morals or the interests of the state, and that is legally prohibited. Crime is criminal activity and those engaged in it. Crime is the habitual or frequent commission of crimes. It is any offense, serious wrongdoing, or sin. It is a foolish, senseless, or shameful act."

Law Enforcement's Definition of Crime

Law enforcement agencies across the country define crime differently from the average citizen. The average citizen sees all crime as bad especially when the criminal activity occurs to us or someone we know. If something is taken from a citizen, they may refer to the crime as a robbery ("I was robbed"). However, that is not always true. For instance, if something is taken from your car that crime is considered theft. If something is taken from your hands or your immediate person that crime is considered a robbery. The point is, a citizen may believe they were robbed however the statistics will reflect the crime was a theft. Crimes are defined in a variety of ways. State laws are defined by state statutes which are voted on by state legislators. County ordinances are voted on by county commissioners and city, or local ordinances are voted on by city councils or local politicians. These statutes and ordinances provide specific descriptions of illegal actions called elements of a crime. These elements are used to determine if there was a violation of the law. For example, a robbery according to Georgia Law, is when a person with the intent to commit a theft takes property of another from the person or immediate presence of another, by force, by intimidation or by sudden snatching. The elements are actions that must be present to constitute a violation of the law. The elements are: (1) intent to commit a theft (in order for there to be a robbery there has to be an intent to take someone's property), (2) the property has to be taken from their person or their immediate presence, (3) the item must be taken by force, (4) intimidation or (5) by sudden snatching. Elements 1 and 2 have to be present, and either 3, 4 or 5 have to be present as well. When these elements come together a robbery has occurred.

Law enforcement agencies also utilize a uniform concept of grouping crimes that seem similar. The program is called Uniform Crime Reporting (UCR). These statistics are compiled by the FBI and disseminated in an annual UCR report. This manner of grouping crimes can provide agencies with a uniform means of reporting crime, so that crime reported in California is reported in the same manner as crime in Alabama. This allows people who compare crime from state to state, city to city or from jurisdiction to jurisdiction in a uniform manner regardless of their definitions by statute. In general, agencies utilize two categories, PART I crimes and PART II crimes. These two groups are then subdivided into various crime groups.

Part I Crimes

Part I crimes include homicide, rape, robbery, aggravated assault, burglary, larceny/theft, motor vehicle theft and arson. These crimes are usually reported to the state by the local departments. For those agencies that participate in the Uniform Crime Reporting (UCR) program, the statistics are also reported to the FBI. Lists that rank states and cities as most or least safe generally determine rankings based on UCR statistics. In some instances, heads of local police departments may report crime in their jurisdiction as decreasing over a certain period of time. The data to support a decrease in crime usually comes from UCR and Part I statistics. In some jurisdictions, Part I crimes are the driving force behind the day to day personnel allocations of a law enforcement agency.

Part II Crimes

These crimes are only reported to the FBI if they result in an arrest. Some examples include vandalism, disorderly conduct, simple battery and public drunkenness. In essence, these Part II crimes are not reported to the FBI unless someone gets arrested for one of those particular crimes. For example, an officer observes someone spray painting graffiti on a wall that is adjacent to a major boulevard. The officer places the suspect under arrest for vandalism at which time the arrest and crime are reported to the FBI. On the other hand, if an officer receives a call for service about graffiti on a wall adjacent to a major boulevard and there is no suspect identified, the officer will simply write a police report. This crime is not reported to the FBI because there was no arrest made. If at some point, a suspect is identified and an arrest is made, the crime would then be reported to the FBI.

> TIP: Information on UCR statistics can be located by going to the Federal Bureau of Investigation website, at FBI.gov.

Allocated Resources

I was at my favorite coffee shop and observed a gentleman sitting near my favorite seat. He was reading a book that appeared to be titled *Criminal Procedures*. I asked him what year he was in school and he stated he was a senior. I told him I was a police officer and criminal procedures was my favorite area within the realm of criminal justice. He asked me was there a difference in the criminal justice classes a college student would attend as compared to criminal justice classes a law enforcement professional would attend. I told him there was a difference. He then asked the difference in civilian criminal justice classes and the training that police officers attend. I explained to him college classes touch on the various theories behind why criminal justice is what it is in addition to theories behind the procedures used within the criminal justice discipline. I went on to explain there is usually very little teaching related to the actual application of those theories. In contrast, law enforcement professionals learn the application of various theories without getting very detailed about the theories themselves. A law enforcement class is more about "this is what we are going to do, and this is how it should be done." Although there is only a little background on the why, which is accomplished by utilizing case law, officers are not engaged in detailed lectures on the actual theories. After explaining the difference in criminal justice classes and police officer training classes he asked, "Why are there more police officers in predominately black communities than there are in the predominately white communities?" I explained law enforcement agencies allocate personnel according to either Part I crimes, political influence, and (or) revenue generation.

Resource Allocation based on Part I Crime

Police officers should frequent areas where crime is highest. Those complaints of theft, rape, robbery, burglary, murder, etc. drive police activity. In the neighborhoods where crime is highest or has the tendency to rise, agencies may maintain a steady flow of directed patrol and anti-crime initiatives.

For example, let's say in a neighborhood, there has been an increase of thefts, robberies, and burglaries. Burglaries usually occur during the daytime when people are at work, but thefts and robberies could occur at any time. Due to this rise in Part I crimes, the agency might increase the number of uniform patrol officers in that community in addition to deploying traffic enforcement units. The additional patrol officers would satisfy an increased uniform presence in the area. Because there is no surplus of trained police officers waiting around, additional officers have to be reassigned from other patrol areas.

The use of specialized units such as a traffic unit is possible especially if there is an area that has garnered complaints of unsafe driving such as speeding or failing to stop at stop signs. These officers might be deployed to conduct a road safety check to quell the unsafe driving in the area. This also adds an additional uniform presence in the area. There could also be an increase in gang unit patrols or specialized crime suppression units. These additional resources depend a lot on public outcry. The allocation of these resources reminds me of an old saying "the squeaky wheel gets the grease." If the community does not show concern for an increase in criminal activity the police department may not make that community the priority that it should be.

The increased visibility of uniform officers in the area usually drives the criminals to another area at which time the cycle begins all over again. To say we are going to stop crime is unrealistic, what is generally done is we address crime by police presence and as a result, it moves to another location. As soon as the officers arrest the bad guy or gal, there are two or three more to take their place, and eventually, those arrested bad guys and gals will be back on the street to do their thing again. As long as there are criminals this dance will continue.

Resource Allocation Based on Political Influence

Political influence is also used to allocate police resources and personnel. There are many decisions in a local jurisdiction that are made based on political associations. I call it "quid pro quo politics". I do something for you, and there is an expectation that in return you will do something for me. Someone who is politically connected in a community can influence the actions of a police department. For example, John Smith is a wealthy restaurateur. John donates food and drinks to the local police department for their annual National Night Out Campaign on a regular basis. John gets a call from a neighbor advising him they will be hosting a big party on this Saturday night, with about 500 expected guests. John picks up the phone, calls the local chief and insists there be officers in the neighborhood to direct traffic on Saturday night. Although the example was fictitious, I'm certain it has occurred somewhere. Political influence can impact who might be issued a traffic citation, who can be placed under arrest and in some instances, who can be released after being stopped for driving under the influence.

Those who have political influence use that influence to get law enforcement agencies to provide extra protection when they feel it is necessary or to avert criminal prosecution. Politics is everywhere! In every local jurisdiction, there is always someone who knows someone, who knows someone. They make phone calls and things happen whether it is the right thing to do or not.

People who have influence make things happen no matter where they are. You do not necessarily have to be rich to have influence or make things happen. People who may have political influence in a community can include those who have a great deal of influence over the people within their community and those who regularly write editorial letters to the local newspaper.

Let's take an arbitrary city in a large metropolitan area. For patrol purposes, the city is divided into six zones (or areas of patrol). Zone one consisted of middle-class, single-family residences and a few businesses. Zone two is made up of government housing or what I call the working poor, single-family homes, homes with elderly heads of households, hotels, and a few restaurants. The residents in zone two did not communicate with city council members, did not attend council meetings, and thus there was no political influence. Zone three is similar to zone two, with the exception of the hotels; however, there are more apartment buildings in zone three. Generally, people who rent apartments and homes do not take an interest in what is going on in their community, thus minimizing their political influence. They are considered transient. Zone four consisted of a downtown business district, middle-class, single-family homes, apartment complexes, and older strip mall type shopping areas. Zone four residents and business owners regularly held community meetings to discuss concerns that needed to be presented to city officials. Zone five is predominately single-family middle, and upper-middle class homes with a couple of apartment complexes and zone six is made up of apartment complexes, businesses, and a few single-family, middle-class homes.

Zone one went through a re-gentrification process that brought more young families to the area. I will call this area the "new" area of zone one, which bordered zone two. Zone two has a significant issue with the sale and use of narcotics and all the ills that drugs bring to a neighborhood. As a result, there began to be a rise in residential burglaries in the "new" area of zone one. The residents became influential in the manner in which they took ownership of their community. Because the "new" area of zone one had influence they demanded police presence increase. These people wrote letters, emails and regularly sat outside their homes to see for themselves if officers patrolled their neighborhood. As a result, the crime was pushed away from the "new" zone one. Any community can do this—it is not difficult, but it takes a commitment. In the chapter titled, "Communication" I talk about how to communicate your community issues with the right people.

Resource Allocation Based on Revenue Generation

Revenue generation is not a new concept. Local and state jurisdictions have been utilizing this as a budget supplement for years. After a Justice Department Review of the Ferguson Police Department, it was determined the city utilized its police department to write citations and make arrests to supplement their general fund.

I worked in a jurisdiction like Ferguson in which officers were encouraged (heavy handed) to increase the number of citations written on a monthly basis. Although there was no formal quota, it was perceived that there had to be a substantial number of citations written each month. In many instances, the citations were tied to promotion and referred to as productivity.

After learning the electric rate (city owned electric company) was one of the highest in the state I refused to write citizens citations for violations such as failing to stop at stop signs and failing to stop at red lights. These citations accompanied up to a $300 fine. There was no way the majority of the city's citizens could pay the fine, electric bill and eat, without having to make payment arrangements which meant being placed on probation. After getting pressured to write more citations I altered the means in which I issued citations. I developed a strong empathy for those residents who paid excessive electric bills and were forced to enter a probation program simply to pay a traffic citation. When faced with writing red light citations and a seatbelt citations I often chose to write only the seatbelt citation, even though the failing to stop for the stop sign or red light was my probable cause for stopping the vehicle. The cost of a stop sign violation and a red light violation was approximately $200-$395, which was incomparable to the $15 seatbelt fine. I explained to the driver that I was only going to write a citation for the seatbelt and would issue a verbal warning for the red light or stop sign violation. This is a great example of a police officer using discretion to help people. Usually I didn't have any problems but there was always someone who wanted to argue they didn't run the light or stop sign, even though I was trying to give them a break. In those situations I was forced to issue them both citations to keep myself out of trouble and being complained on. I issued them both citations and encouraged them to go to court to argue. I never stopped anyone unjustly. There was always a violation if I stopped a vehicle and I always advised the driver why they were being stopped. If they were pleasant I went back to my vehicle and returned with a seatbelt citation. If they were belligerent or rude I would return with the citation for the probable cause in which they were stopped.

Officers had certain areas they surveyed to get their productivity. Some chose to write traffic citations, and others chose to write criminal citations or take people to jail. I chose traffic lights and stop signs while still performing my patrol duties. Some police officers might refer to these certain areas of their patrol beat, as "target rich environments." These "target rich environments" are places an officer might visit to frequently write citations, which eventually will generate revenue for the jurisdiction. An example of a target rich environment, that officers used as a revenue generator, is a local state route that I frequent on my way to work. At the bottom of the hill, the police stand on the sidewalk and shoot their lasers towards the top of the hill identifying speeders. By the time the driver notices the police on the side of the road, they are met by an officer standing in the middle of the street flagging the driver down to stop. This is not a black/white issue, but a green one. It is about writing as many tickets as possible as fast as the officer can. The same could be said for a drug-infested neighborhood. There is a potential to arrest drug users, drug sellers, people loitering to buy drugs, people loitering to commit thefts and people violating traffic laws. It is a target rich environment, so the police are going to be there. If this were my community, I would want the police there as well.

 I know what you are thinking: "So, there aren't any drugs in the more affluent neighborhoods?" Of course, there are drugs in the affluent neighborhoods, but you don't see folks standing on the corner, waiting for a car to pull up do you? No, of course not. If that happened, everyone would know there were drugs in the community, the residents would move, and it would no longer be an affluent community. The affluent folks leave their suburban communities and go to the inner cities, or they arrange for a meeting somewhere unsuspecting. Usually when some affluent kid becomes so addicted to drugs and they can no longer get mom and dad to unknowingly support their habit, they begin to take things from around the house and then around the neighborhood. They tend to steal in a manner that avoids detection. There is always an explanation for missing trinkets around the house. If one of these affluent teens does get caught taking something that does not belong to them, the enabling parent jumps in to save them by making a phone call to an attorney or the store manager. Generally, there is some deal for restitution before the police even arrive. When they escalate to breaking into other homes or robbing stores, they usually do not commit these crimes in their neighborhoods. The risk of being caught and the embarrassment to them and their families are far too great.

Drug use is a personal choice that can escalate to dependency. Although possession, use, manufacturing and distributing drugs are all criminal offenses, I am not concerned with someone and their drug abuse as long as it does not interfere with my quality of life. When drug use interferes with someone's quality of life I believe they should contact the police and allow them to generate some revenue and clean up the neighborhood. If you do decide to call, *beware* and be ready for an increase in police activity in your neighborhood. This means make certain that you are stopping at every stop sign, carrying your driver's license, wearing your seatbelt, and obeying every other law and ordinance there is. It is not that they are coming after you for complaining, but rather, they are giving you the visibility that is needed in the area. The police should not discriminate in how they enforce the law. Therefore, you will be expected to adhere to all applicable laws and ordinances just as the people you complained about. When you call, the police will develop a plan to address the issues you are concerned about. If the solution is a safety checkpoint, then so be it, just make sure you are following the law.

Politician's Definition of Crime

The laws police and sheriff departments are charged with enforcing are state law, county ordinances and (or) city ordinances. These laws are often proposed by state representatives and state senators who use their personal reasons and/or suggestions and/or complaints from constituents. After finding their way through the legislative process, these proposed bills sometimes become actual state statutes. This same process occurs in county commissions and city councils. They develop an ordinance proposal; there are public comments and time to amend the ordinance or make changes to it before it is voted on. Then it is either passed as an ordinance or not. When these laws and ordinances become effective, it is the duty of the applicable law enforcement agency to enforce those laws. Therefore, if you live in the city limits you will have to abide by city ordinances and state laws, the county ordinances are still applicable as well. If you live outside the city limits, there are no city ordinances that will govern you so you should be safe being familiar with the state laws and county ordinances. Knowing all city ordinances, county ordinances and state laws is a pretty large feat. I believe it would be satisfactory to simply be aware of where to find the information.

You should also be aware that the laws vary from state to state. For example, wearing a handgun on your hip may be legal in one state but illegal in another. Ignorance of the law is *no excuse*! When traveling, you should not only know the touristy places to visit but also what laws apply to you while you are there. If you desire to take your handgun with you, you should know if you can carry it, what documentation you might need to carry it, and how the law says you have to carry it. I cannot say or express this any more clearly: "*Ignorance of the law is not a defense*." In plain English, saying, "I didn't know that was a law," does not mean that you will not get a ticket nor does it mean that you won't get arrested. Some people who are issued citations or placed under

> TIP: Municode.com is a great reference for municipal ordinances.

arrest simply did not know they were breaking the law.

Now, of course, I'm aware that some laws are enforced in

> TIP: The following states recognize and reciprocate in recognizing the Georgia firearms license:
>
> Alabama, Alaska, Arizona, Arkansas, Colorado, Florida, Idaho, Indiana, Iowa, Kansas, Kentucky, Louisiana, Maine, Michigan, Mississippi, Missouri, Montana, New Hampshire, North Carolina, North Dakota, Ohio, Oklahoma, Pennsylvania, South Carolina, South Dakota, Tennessee, Texas, Utah, West Virginia, Wisconsin, Wyoming

some places but not in others. For example, going back to the various patrol areas, let's say zone two may be considered a high crime area, but there are also hotels and restaurants in zone two. The average income and education level is a bit lower in areas of zone two. In contrast, zone one has areas with more educated middle-class citizens. And let's say there is a city ordinance that prohibits public drinking. I believe, and this is my own opinion, that this sort of ordinance would be in place to keep people from drinking and being drunk on the public streets, but this may not be how the ordinance is enforced. Generally, in zone two, officers wrote citations and arrested people for drinking on private property. That is correct; officers observed people having a cold beer while in their yard or someone else's yard and initiated contact with them. This is usually just a reason they used to conduct an illegal search for drugs. They get a ticket for drinking in public unless they agreed to go through a search of their pockets. If drugs were found, they were arrested. Depending on the officer they probably would not get a ticket for the beer because it was just a reason to stop them. In contrast, the same ordinance is applicable in zone one, but it was not enforced on people walking on the public sidewalks drinking beer from beer bottles. If you are having a cold beer while cutting your grass and the police harass you about it, complain in writing!

The People's Definition of Crime

Last, but not least, crime is defined by us, "the people." How do we define crime? Usually, we do not even think about what crime is or how much of it there is until it directly or indirectly impacts us. Meaning, unless we, or someone we know, is robbed or assaulted or their home is burglarized, we don't really care that there is crime or how it is defined. Our experiences with the law and law enforcement dictate the level of knowledge we have. If we receive a traffic citation for failure to stop at a stop sign we generally take the officer's word that we didn't stop or we argue that we did stop, but how many times do we do the research to find out just what that law says? So, if you do not take the time to find out what the failure to stop at a stop sign law actually says, then you will find yourself at the mercy of the court. You may be found guilty of the violation unless the officer fails to show up on the court date or some other procedural issue occurs.

We have to take responsibility to report crime even when it doesn't directly impact us. If you see something, you should report it. If you are inside your home and you see someone walking down the street carrying a large television. You should call the police. It was someone else's home that was burglarized today, but tomorrow it could be yours. Is it fair for someone to ask for help when their family member is a victim of crime, while withholding information about other crimes?

How about this example, you are aware of a group who regularly shoplifts expensive clothes, purses, and shoes from a local mall but you say nothing. Weeks later someone shoots and kills a family member of yours, and you go on the news asking for people with information to come forward. Is it right that you have information about a theft that occurred, but say nothing? Yet you expect people to come forward with information about the killing of your family member. No, it is not right, even though shoplifting is not comparable to someone's death there is still a loss. The store that was victimized has to overcome the loss. The cost will be passed on to paying consumers, or the business may decide it is just not profitable to remain in the area. Police agencies have made providing information about criminal activity easier and in some instances profitable. Simply use the anonymous tip lines. You do not have to leave your name. If we want people to "snitch" for us, we should be willing to "snitch" for others. You should not be able to have it both ways. The same should be said for police officers.

Community influence is evident at election time. The failure to go to the polls and vote is an indication of a community's disinterest in not only the political process but also for the laws that are passed on their behalf. The voting process is used to elect people to office who have the community's best interest in mind. To elect people who are going to propose and pass laws that reflect what you care about and believe in. When someone fails to vote it means your team gets zero and the other team gets one. Even when you fail to vote, it still counts. At this time everyone has the right to vote; however, there are barriers being put in place to make voting, for some, difficult. Be a part of the process. Do not just stand by and allow laws to be made that you must obey without being a part of the process. You cannot learn the game if you are not involved in the rule-making process and you certainly do not have the right to complain about laws if you do not take an active participation in electing responsible, intelligent people who have your best interest in mind.

Enforcing the Laws of the Land

Although there are many tasks that encompass the job of a police officer one of the most important is providing a safe environment for citizens free of criminal activity by enforcing the laws of the land. This enforcement of laws is accomplished very differently depending on the community you live. There have been a number of initiatives by law enforcement management executives to accomplish this task, such as zero-tolerance policing, community policing and problem oriented policing. All of these initiatives are an effort to combat crime and return communities to the safe environments we all deserve, but often the methods used can be devastating to a community.

In 1982 James Wilson and George Kelling introduced the Broken Windows Theory. The theory uses a broken window as a metaphor to describe disorder and incivility within neighborhoods (McKee, A.J.). The theory goes on to link this disorder and incivility to the propensity of criminal activity. The Broken Windows Theory states it is necessary to address disorder within a community to prevent fear and withdrawal of citizens within the community (Center for Evidence-Based Crime Policy).

Law enforcement management officials have applied this theory to policing by enforcing small infractions, so they do not become more serious criminal offenses. Some departments refer to the smaller infractions as quality of life issues. For example, a patrol officer might enforce loitering laws by warning people not to linger in various areas. People "hanging out" in front of a convenience store might discourage people from patronizing that business causing the owner a hardship. That same group may lead to robberies of pedestrians in the area or potential business robberies. Enforcing loitering laws, in theory, may deter these types of crimes.

Traffic enforcement is a means to deter criminal activity. Speed detection deters people from speeding as you cannot anticipate when an officer might be in the area enforcing speeding laws, which modifies the speeding behavior and encourages traveling at the posted speed limit. Enforcing minor traffic violations such as equipment violations can deter people from frequenting certain areas.

Some law enforcement agencies have utilized zero-tolerance policing under the guise of broken windows policing. Zero-tolerance policing is still subjective, but the point is to punish violators for any infraction of the law to modify behavior and create a more law abiding community. Zero-tolerance policing has led to a number of people, mostly minorities arrested for minor infractions. There has been mass incarceration of entire races. The police blame the criminal element for the problem, "if they were obeying the law they would not have been arrested" or the citizens blame the police in that there is no application of empathy in the enforcement of laws, "*everyone* has to go to jail it's zero-tolerance."

A second unintended problem with zero-tolerance policing is taking discretion away from the officer on the scene, preventing them from considering the circumstances at hand. Zero-tolerance policing can also cause officers to look the other way rather than address minor criminal infractions.

Finally, a third unintended effect of zero-tolerance policing is the toll it takes on the people who live in the community. Residents who implore the police to make their communities safe are also victims of zero-tolerance policing. They receive citations and get arrested just as the people they complain about. The ongoing "putting the foot down" of the police takes a mental, financial and physical toll on citizens who are involved in minor infractions of the law.

Zero-tolerance traffic enforcement can be used to address minor traffic infractions and equipment violations to deter drug offenses, burglaries, robberies, etc. For example, a vehicle travels into an area in which officers have made several arrests for the sale and purchase of illegal narcotics. That vehicle has a brake light out. Generally, state laws are specific in stating the two brake lights on the rear of each side of the vehicle must be operational. An officer on patrol notices the brake light out, initiates a traffic stop and issues a citation. The driver, after receiving a citation for such a minor infraction may think twice about entering that neighborhood, thus minimizing the chance that they would return for criminal activity.

My first policing job was in a small city outside of Atlanta. I lived there for a little over a year and noticed the utilities, which were provided by the city had higher rates than the larger providers in the area. Our police department began zero-tolerance policing. We were told to "increase our productivity" which meant to write more tickets and make more arrests. The call for increased productivity was to address increases in thefts and burglaries in the city but it also helped the city's general fund.

2
THE POLICE

Rule 2: *All police officers are not created the same. Some have different motivations than others. Knowing various personalities of those who protect and serve us can help us understand how to interact with law enforcement personnel.*

We have seen these men and women in uniform in our neighborhoods, on the news, in transportation hubs, at coffee shops, and, yes, even a donut shop every now and then, but who are they? Police officers are people. They are human beings; the same as you and I. These individuals have also answered a calling to protect and serve our communities, which sometimes involves placing themselves in harm's way for people they do not know. These officers range in age from 18 to 80. They represent each and every facet of this melting pot we call the United States of America. Police officers come from a variety of different backgrounds, including race, ethnicity, gender and sexual orientation. According to The United States Department of Justice, Office of Justice Programs *Bureau of Justice Statistics Report (2013),* today's law enforcement agencies in the United States are more diverse than in 2007, comprising of 72.8% White officers, 12.2% Black officers, 11.6% Latino officers and 2.4% Asian/Native Hawaiian/other Pacific Islander officers. Although there has been an increase in minority representation in law enforcement, the increase since 2007 has been minimal. From 2007 to 2013 there was a total minority increase of 2% with only a 5%

increase in Black officers. These officers represent different countries and have different levels of education, values, and beliefs that form their professional, political, and social viewpoints.

In a time when there is so much division in our country and such a rift between law enforcement and a variety of communities, it is important that we remind ourselves that these officers are human and just as corporate workers make mistakes in the course of their jobs, law enforcement officers will make mistakes as well. Because there are mistakes made by law enforcement officers that can result in the loss of life or serious bodily injury, repetitive, effective training is vital. Although it is very difficult to train officers for each and every scenario that may be encountered, it is imperative that training is relevant, consistent and ongoing to effect the change communities are demanding.

Community policing is a concept that has been evolving since the 1970's. The community policing model was not truly an acceptable means of handling the ills of the streets until approximately 20 years later in 1990's. There was a stigma that accompanied the title "Community Oriented Policing Officer." The words that most often described officers who were assigned to community oriented policing units were, soft, lazy and apprehensive. They were considered too soft to patrol the rough streets and were sometimes assigned to community policing to save them from being injured or causing some other officer to be injured. In some departments, a community policing unit was where they hid or punished "lazy" officers. These were officers who did not make enough arrests or write enough citations.

Today community policing is seen more as an overall method in addressing community ills, rather than a simple unit comprised of two or three officers. In addition to the increased use of community policing strategies with all patrol officers there is less need for a community policing unit. Some police departments across the country have approached crisis mode in identifying and developing viable officer candidates. Because of officer shortages, departments are placing officers who were hidden in office roles back on the streets in a patrol function. The issue with removing officers from an office role to patrol is some may have lost or forgotten the street knowledge they had prior to entering the office role. Moreover, they may have had limited exposure to relevant patrol training since being in the office role. I can recall a calculus professor who encouraged working through problems and proofs during vacation so that we did not lose the concepts we had previously learned. The saying, "If you do not use it you will lose it is true." It is true in mathematics just as it is true in law enforcement. Those departments that hid apprehensive, lazy officers in community policing units found those officers being promoted or reassigned to field positions at various stages in their careers. The department was adding experienced officers to the field, but those officers and supervisors lacked the tools needed to be effective in those positions. Officers who settle into positions for long periods of time sometimes fail to grow and continue their development. They get comfortable with the routine and develop a laissez-faire mindset of "well this is the way we used to do it, so that is the way I will keep doing it." It is very difficult for police officers and police managers to accept change. I worked for a police department that still, as of 2016, wrote police reports using pen and paper.

Types of Officers

The rank and file officers, the beat officers you see every day, generally have one common goal and that is to return home in the same or better condition than when they arrived at work. When it comes down to it, police officers do what it takes to get home safe to their families. Every day before a shift an officer may have a thought in the back of their mind that "something could happen today to prevent me from going home". This thought, no matter how faint or strong influences an officer's response to a variety of situations. I would feel safe in saying it is this belief that provokes a use of force or encourages excessive force rather than the thought of seeking people out to harm them.

I truly do not feel the majority of police officers would chance the negative public scrutiny, risk of criminal prosecution and the financial burden that comes with being involved in an incident that results in the death or serious bodily injury of a citizen; simply because they did not "like" someone or because they did not "like" the way someone looked or because they did not "like" how someone acted. However, there are always exceptions. There are bad apples in every department. They are well known and popular. Their arrogant and sometimes aggressive behavior is evident. Remember these officers do not change, they are who they are. These officers work hard and achieve results. They patrol their beat every single day letting everyone know they are in charge. These are generally officers who request to work in high crime areas. In some instances, these areas of town have lower education levels, and the citizens are less likely to complain. Police managers also tend to place these officers in these type of communities because they know anywhere else will garner citizen complaints. These officers get promoted, they train new officers, they become supervisors and decision makers. This one officer can create a culture within a department that breeds unprofessionalism, misconduct, and mistreatment of certain citizens.

    Police officers have been tasked with many more responsibilities than enforcing the laws of the land. Officers respond to calls for service in which they are expected to counsel adults who may be having domestic issues, counsel children in the importance of attending school regularly, identifying and seeking treatment for mentally disabled individuals, all while attempting to maintain their own personal relationships. These types of counseling situations are often performed by licensed individuals who are required to endure years of school and professional certification requirements. Although police officers complete a certification program, they are not licensed sociologists, psychologists or psychiatrists, yet a major duty of American law enforcement officers is counseling.

Police officers are often exposed to problems, conflict, stress, physical aggression, loss of a colleague, murder, rape, robbery, child abuse and molestation while on duty. The day to day incidents that officers endure along with the overnight shifts, rotating shifts, inconsistent sleeping patterns and the inability to spend quality time with family can all be additional stressors for an officer. The impact of this stress can manifest professionally, with increased aggression, increased cynicism, alcoholism, drug abuse and increased citizen complaints. These stressors can also impact the officer's personal life, causing difficulty with family relations, isolation, divorce and thoughts of suicide. Research in 2003, by Corey Haines, indicated the national divorce rate was 50%; however the rate among police officers was 60-75%.

Police officers mourn just like any other group but, in my opinion, mourning an officer killed in the line of duty is especially difficult. If an officer has been on the job for any amount of time, they probably have had the unfortunate opportunity to attend the funeral of a Fallen Officer. I have been to many funerals of loved ones and friends, but there is none sadder, more touching, and more heartfelt than the funeral of an officer who was killed in the line of duty, even one you had no personal relationship with. The thought that an officer was killed because someone did not want to go to jail is ridiculous. The hard, honest truth is that the officer does not know you. Upon first glance, they cannot distinguish you from a serial murderer or a kindergarten teacher. Of course, we go through training classes that are supposed to help us discern between the good guys and the bad guys, but in that mix are their own personal beliefs, values, and experiences and in some instances, the picture gets a little cloudy.

Sheepdog Cops

There are some officers who believe in the sheepdog mentality. This is a mindset that some officers have about the people they protect and serve and how they fit into that equation. A herd of sheep is considered vulnerable and unaware of the harm that sometimes lurks in the shadows. The sheepdog is recruited to protect those sheep. They are recruited to ensure the sheep can continue to walk around with no worries that predators may have the thought of preying upon them. Those officers who take on this mentality feel their job is to watch over the citizens, the sheep.

They protect you while you shop, your homes while you're at work, and as you sleep soundly throughout the night. No need to worry—the "sheepdog" is on duty. The sheepdog officer will go over and beyond to ensure their sheep are protected. These officers are always on duty. The issue lies when the "cop" on the beat loses that sheepdog mentality. They forget why they do what they do. They forget about protecting the sheep. They lose the desire to work for the people. The cynicism takes over, and they fall prey to the unfairness of departmental politics. The department they thought was great when they applied turns out to have nepotism, favoritism, or the "good old boy or girl" problem. The inability to make ends meet without working two or more jobs becomes overwhelming. The desire to be promoted becomes the new priority rather than patrolling their beat ensuring the sheep remain protected. This effort to seek more money and departmental power tends to make us forget why we took the job.

Corporate Officer

Law enforcement of the past was comprised of type A males, military types, and athletes who were not able to make it to professional leagues. Later came type A women and former college athletes who were unable to play professional sports overseas. There was also a lack of women's professional sports in the United States. The education requirement was usually met by graduating from high school, although some agencies only required a General Education Development Certificate (GED). Some agencies developed hiring processes that included stringent physical fitness tests. There was a strong paramilitary structure within these agencies.

The push for law enforcement to become a profession created opportunities for people who were not enlisted in the military or former athletes. Agencies actively recruited people with college degrees and offered them higher starting salaries than those without college degrees. Law enforcement departments began to be more diverse in racial and gender makeup. Law enforcement provided a career in which candidates believed they would see lots of action and each day would be filled with excitement.

Today law enforcement has continued to move away from the strict paramilitary style of old. Although the ranking structure may remain, law enforcement has evolved into a new, more technological, intelligence gathering, professional entity that values and embraces the concept of community policing. This new type of law enforcement requires a different type of officer, a different type of supervisor, and most importantly a different type of police chief. The requirements for law enforcement agencies have slowly begun to change from anyone being able to apply to a minimum of a GED, then a minimum of a high school diploma and, in some agencies now, a minimum requirement of two years of college. The move simply aligns law enforcement with the theory that a more educated officer is more equipped to handle the demands of today's police job. Those critical thinking skills that are necessary to complete a college program are indeed necessary to perform the complicated tasks of today's police officer. When you really think about it, we ask the police to be psychologists, psychiatrists, counselors, doctors, and lawyers but law enforcement is one profession that does not REQUIRE a specialized degree.

After the terrorist attack of 9/11 and then the recession that followed, thousands of people quit their corporate jobs to serve their country. Those who were not eligible or willing to join the military applied for law enforcement related jobs. During the recession, there were many people who were laid off from their corporate jobs, at the same time college students graduated with no hope of employment in their chosen fields, simultaneously, more and more men and women were leaving the military. They were all looking for employment and turned to police related jobs.

Economic instability, home foreclosures rising at astonishing rates and a rise in unemployment became catalysts in the increase of crime in certain areas. Fortunately, the law enforcement community had a sort of perfect storm. There was a multitude of talented people to pick from, like corporate security professionals, engineers, and teachers. This opportunity to pick officer candidates from such diverse talents, at the same time that crime was increasing, allowed police agencies across the country to build more knowledgeable, professional ranks, just in time.

The influx of "corporate ways" diluted the paramilitary processes of the "Old Police." "*The way it used to be*" is now the mantra of many police officers. As stated earlier, the minimum requirements have changed, and departments are looking for more educated personnel to deal with the variety of technological changes in law enforcement.

In the past a chief of just about any department, large or small, was generally promoted up the ranks in the same department **HE** started **HIS** career with. Supervisors and managers were generally good friends of the chief. They were people who were proven trustworthy. Chiefs of Police of larger departments are now located utilizing nationwide searches. These candidates are not just white males any longer but rather a diverse field that often reflects the communities they serve. They come with abundant credentials including college degrees and Federal, State, and (or) local management training. Today, it is not good enough to have worked hard, performed your duties above expectations, served with loyalty, and ascended the ranks by performing various assignments within a department. You have to be affiliated with the right people, be in the right click, and have the right credentials. You have to be confident, but not too confident, knowledgeable, but not too knowledgeable and you must also be aware of those political influences such as your affiliating political party, church affiliation and other aspects of your social life.

Adrenaline Junkie Officer

As stated earlier, people get into law enforcement for a variety of reasons. Some are adrenaline junkies and are looking for that constant action. These *adrenaline junkie officers* tend to get in trouble more often than any other officer. These are the officers, who after perusing their internal affairs file, are found to have documentation of numerous incidents involving uses of force in addition to citizen complaints. The average cop show is on television for about one hour with about fifteen to twenty minutes of commercials. The entire show is filled with some cop involved in a lot of action. The shows depict action in every minute of the program and ends with the case being solved.

In real life, it is not like that at all. Real world policing is riding or walking around, waiting for something to happen, and listening to people's problems, like why Johnny took the keys when his wife was trying to leave to go to work or why little Jimmie didn't go to school today. Every once in a while you might respond to something action packed like a robbery or shooting, something to get your adrenaline flowing, but for the most part, you are on edge just waiting on something to happen.

These "adrenaline junkie" officers have to be on edge. They have to have something going on. If they are not responding to action filled calls for service they try to create their own action. I have seen these type of officers approach citizens asking them if they have anything on them and then rummaging through their pockets with no authority to do so, clearly violating the citizen's rights. The following example is one that is prevalent with adrenaline junkie officers: An officer approaches of a group of young men standing near the corner in front of one of the young men's home and tells them all to disperse and move on. When the group fails to leave the officer exits the vehicle and begins to ask for identification. One of the males flees because he knows he has a marijuana cigarette in his pocket. The officer gives chase, involves other officers and at last the "suspect" is apprehended. A search is conducted, but the marijuana cigarette is not located. The officer asks the man why he ran but the man refused to answer and remained silent. This is your right. The officer charges the man with obstruction and takes him to jail. There was no probable cause for the stop. The men were not obstructing the sidewalk, and there was no law that stated they could not gather in front of the man's home. Obstruction is a bad charge in this scenario. Although an officer can give chase when there is at least reasonable articulable suspicion that a crime may be occurring or about to occur, based on the totality of the circumstances; however merely gathering in front of a home is not a crime and there was no articulation that a crime was about to occur. There is nothing wrong with patrolling your beat; however to chase someone for simply running, upon sight of the police can be a dangerous action. It can be dangerous to the police officer, dangerous to the person running and dangerous to those officers responding for assistance.

It should be noted; it is not necessarily against the law to walk away or run from a police officer. BUT if an officer has reasonable belief that criminal activity is occurring they can stop the fleeing person (investigatory stop) to determine if there is probable cause for the stop. The example in a United States Supreme Court Case, *Illinois v Wardlow*, provides the example. Officers approached Wardlow in a neighborhood that was "known for heavy drug activity." Wardlow fled, officers gave chase, located Wardlow and conducted a pat down for weapons, at which time they located a gun. The gun provided the probable cause officers needed for the arrest. There are several pieces of case law that were applied in determining this case, such as *Adams v. Williams*, which is applied to the characteristics of the location and *United States v. Brignoni-Ponce*, which was applied to the nervous characteristics of a suspect. The lesson learned here is if someone runs from the police they can be chased but there are other circumstances that have to occur, and the officer has to be able to articulate those circumstances when making a lawful arrest. While it is good to know case law that guides officers in the performance of their duties it is not a good idea to recite case law while the officer is conducting their investigation. Throwing case law and other legal jargon in the face of officers at the time you are being stopped can make a situation worse. Either the officer may be unaware of case law that pertains to how they perform their duties or they do know it and resent you knowing it. Knowledge is power, but you have to know how to use it.

Running from the police opens you up to a myriad of other issues that depend on the integrity of the officer chasing you. We would love to assume that the officer chasing us is filled with honesty and integrity. You should not give an officer an opportunity to spin the situation in a manner that provides them probable cause based on something they "thought" they saw. If you have done nothing wrong, there is no reason to run. Running makes the entire situation worse. Running may lead to a use of force that could lead to excessive force. Running to avoid being arrested for a simple warrant could result in the loss of life or serious bodily injury, whether it was a result of falling, the application of an electro-shock device or being shot by a gun. None of these outcomes are worth the punishment that you would face for the crime.

The adrenaline junkie is looking for excitement. They are looking to use force. They are looking for a fight. If you know this ahead of time, you will know how to respond to them. Stay calm, listen to what they are saying and act accordingly. Mentally document the encounter and make a written complaint after the encounter is over. If you do not write well, take someone with you to ensure your complaint is documented clearly. The same behavior can be applied to a traffic stop. If an officer approaches your vehicle, with aggression, meet that aggression with calmness. Again, mentally document the encounter, if it was a negative encounter, make a written complaint.

The Ease by Officer

The *ease by officer* is a person who just wants to ride the clock. They may have a little professional experience in some other field, a little education, but maybe found they were unable to meet the measurable standards that were required in their previous positions. The law enforcement job is one that provides an officer the freedom to walk or ride around without stringent supervision. It is very hard to micromanage a police officer, which is why departments look for officers who have integrity, are self-motivated, self-disciplined and honest.

These ease by officers are sometimes seen sitting in patrol cars behind abandoned buildings watching a movie, on their Facebook or Twitter accounts, or even sleeping. Some even go shopping while on duty. When I was in my field training program I was told a good patrol officer patrols their beat with the windows down. It is imperative for an officer to be able to use all of their senses, while on patrol. It is difficult for an officer to hear or smell anything with the windows up. While I understand an officer taking a break from driving and resting in the parking lot of a business I cannot understand sitting there with the windows up.

These officers sometimes give management a difficult time about measurable productivity. (It should be noted that quotas are unlawful.) They are the first to rebuke any attempts of management to encourage more proactive activities of their police officers. These officers are supposed to be patrolling your neighborhood and answering your calls for service. These types of officers sometimes make excuses to get out of work or make up absurd stories to get out of taking reports. An example would be: An elderly lady called the police to report something was taken from her porch. She called to get a police report made, but the responding officer told her that she was only eligible for two reports a year and she shouldn't waste one on something like this. Of course, the elderly lady decided not to have a report taken on that occasion. Another example, a male requested a police report because his bicycle was stolen. The officer told him he was unable to take the report because the man did not have proof that he owned the bicycle. The man was told to leave and return with proof that he owned the bicycle before he could provide him with a police report. Another example was when a female contacted the police because her phone was snatched from her hands. The officer told the female there was no reason to make a report because the suspect was not going to be caught and her phone was not going to be located.

Be aware of the ease by officer. They may discourage you from doing something like making a police report that you will need later. For instance, to get replacement phones, you need a police report. To report credit card fraud, you need a police report. If the officer refuses to give you a police report, you will eventually have to return for one. Recognize who this officer is, if you are not satisfied with the response of the officer, ask for a supervisor. If you are still not satisfied, make a written complaint.

The Community Police Officer

This officer should not be confused with the officer, who is assigned to a community policing unit. This officer is one who genuinely cares for the people in the community they patrol. They have a legitimate concern for the safety, security, health, and welfare of all of the people in the community. They patrol the neighborhood with the windows down; they may exit the vehicle to speak with members of the community about their concerns. They provide suggestions to solve those issues. They provide resources such as phone numbers and persons to contact for government agencies. They are seen in the streets playing with children and giving advice about being successful in school. They are not simply there to make arrests and write citations. They develop relationships with the community members that garner a mutual respect. This mutual respect assists the officers in performing their duties with ease. When you get to know people, you generally know how they react to situations, allowing the officer and the citizen the ability to communicate with understanding and trust. There appears to be an ongoing dilemma in the assignment of officers to particular areas and how long to assign them there. There are benefits and consequences of both. Positive benefits are those mentioned above, the development of trust and increased communication between an officer who has been assigned to a community for an extended period, provided their personality allows them to be an officer who exudes trust and is capable of effective communication, with any type of person. The extended assignment of an officer who is not one that exudes trust and who is not capable of communicating with any type of person is not a community centered officer, and they have the potential to create problems with community members. The officer who may be described as an ease by officer or adrenaline junkie officer being assigned to a neighborhood for an extended period could be detrimental to the community and their relationship with the police department. Their mere presence can create a perception of the police that is one other than the community centered philosophy that a department may be attempting to cast upon the neighborhood.

Professionalism

The manner in which an officer approaches a citizen speaks volumes. For example, an officer may greet a citizen on the street who appears to be lost or troubled, saying "How are you today? "Can I help you with anything?" Although this greeting is very professional and unobtrusive, the officer may be attempting to find out why the citizen has been standing in a specific location for an extended period. Even though there is a legitimate reason to stop the citizen, the officer's approach is professional. With a professional approach from the officer, the citizen is expected to respond in a courteous, honest and forthcoming manner. Their behavior is mirroring the professional demeanor of the officer.

A negative approach by an officer generally elicits the potential for a negative citizen response. For example, given the same situation, the officer asks, "What are you doing here? I need to see your ID." The response could be opposite of the more courteous citizen response. Rather than being truthful and forthcoming with information, the citizen may respond by being very defensive and resentful, resulting in a negative police/citizen encounter. Rather than hearing "Can I help you?" the citizen may now hear "What the hell are you doing here?" Because the officer has to control the situation they then may become more aggressive in their response to the citizen's negative response. Regardless of a citizen's reaction, the officer should remain professional although sometimes they do not. These encounters have the potential to turn from that of determining why a citizen is at the location to the citizen being taken to jail. The point here is sometimes rude, unprofessional behavior can turn a pretty simple encounter into one that lasts longer than necessary with consequences that were unintended, like someone being arrested and taken to jail.

In any encounter, a professional officer should use their knowledge, training, and experience to determine if a law was broken or if someone was actually in need of their assistance when determining if it is lawful to extend a police/citizen encounter. If there was probable cause to make an arrest the officer should make the arrest and move on. If there was a citizen who needed assistance, the officer should assist and move on. A police officer's professionalism is important in depicting a positive perception for all law enforcement officers and not just the officer who is involved in the encounter. Moreover, an unprofessional officer provides a negative perception of all law enforcement regardless of how "good" other officers are.

The successful participation of police officers in quality college educational programs are an important ingredient in citizen/police encounters. From 1931 until 1978, numerous commissions called for increased educational requirements of police officers, including a proposed mandate for Bachelor's degrees. The Commissions included: the 1931 Wickersham Commission, the 1967 President's Commission on Law Enforcement and the Administration of Justice also, the 1968 National Advisory Commission on Civil Disorders, the 1969 National Commission on the Causes and Prevention of Violence, the 1972 American Bar Association on Standards for Criminal Justice, the 1973 National Advisory Commission on Criminal Justice Standards and Goals and the 1978 Police Foundation's Advisory Commission on Higher Education for Police Officers.

Research has shown that college educated officers have better communication skills, write better reports, are more tolerant with citizens, have a better understanding of policing and the criminal justice system and have a better comprehension of civil rights issues from multiple perspectives. These officers are more apt to view situations with an open mind in addition to utilizing critical thinking skills in their decisions. These skills are important to police officers because they are called upon by a diverse population to provide advice, mediate disputes and make life and death decisions.

Each work day police officers gather their uniform, badge, gun and head out into our communities to make important decisions that impact the present and future lives of everyday citizens. In most situations, these decisions are made without the assistance of a supervisor. In my experience as a beat officer, there were very few occasions when an officer waited on a supervisor to make a decision. Generally, the supervisor did not show up until the decision was made. Beat officers had to have the knowledge of the law to make valid arrests. The supervisor usually only showed up to sign the police report. In other departments a supervisor may respond to decide if someone should go to jail or not. In those type of departments if an officer got it wrong and placed someone under arrest and there was no probable cause to arrest, the officer may be told to complete a person detained report in an effort to try to justify the mistake. This was common practice in one department; the officers sometimes did not have the knowledge, training or experience to make a simple arrest and neither did the supervisor. Officers have to have a clear understanding of criminal procedure and the statutes they are charged with enforcing. This doesn't come from college course work, but a thorough all-encompassing training program that utilizes knowledgeable, experienced and proactive training officers.

My experience with a couple of different departments has provided me with an opinion that places great value on training. When experienced, proactive training officers are involved in training new officers, they tend to learn more and thus make better decisions. When new officers are trained by training officers, who are not proactive and lacking in the knowledge necessary to make adequate decisions regarding arrests there tends to be a rippling effect that impacts the decisions of the department as a whole. The new officers who were poorly trained become poorly trained training officers, they are then promoted to poorly trained supervisors and then promoted to poorly trained managers. This creates a culture of officers, supervisors, and managers who are poorly trained. As the person ascends to each higher level, they tend to mirror the behavior and actions that were displayed by the person who held the position previously. If the culture of the department condones a philosophy of "I had to figure it out on my own, so you figure it out on your own," rather than a philosophy of mentorship and coaching the culture will continue to be one with inadequately trained officers who make poor decisions.

Excessive use of force is another display of unprofessionalism. The use of force is defined by the International Association of Police Chiefs as "the amount of effort required by police to compel compliance by an unwilling subject." The proverbial jury is still out on excessive use of force. The means of reporting and what is reported from law enforcement agencies allows inconsistent interpretations of what excessive use of force actually is. Recently state and local agencies have had to pay civil damages as a result of excessive use of force litigation. This litigation is often tied to the failure of officers to follow department policies and procedures. Reasons for the payment of civil damages as opposed to criminal prosecution is due to a lower threshold of liability compared to the threshold of guilt in criminal proceedings. Another possible reason for the lack of criminal prosecution is the *Objective Reasonableness Test* provided by the United States Supreme Court case *Graham v Connor*. In *Graham v Connor*, The Court decided in determining whether an incident of force was reasonable it should be judged on objective reasonableness. Further it should be based on all of the circumstances. The decision should also be based on what a reasonable **_officer_** would do in that same situation.

The force an officer uses should be reasonable. But, who defines reasonable? Reasonable depends on the details of each situation. Reasonableness should not be applied as a cookie cutter to all incidents. What might be a reasonable response by an officer to one incident cannot and should not be applied to all incidents. There are many factors, such as the experience of the officer, environment, the age of the officer, the age of the offender, physical capabilities of the officer and that of the offender, time of day and on and on and on. These factors impact how an officer responds to an incident.

An officer who is unable to control their emotions can potentially make detrimental decisions in situations where force is necessary. Officers who are lacking maturity and self-control may find themselves in situations where excessive use of force is an everyday occurrence. I refer to these officers as the *bullied*. They are the officers who joined the force to wear a badge and gun and exert their *authority*. This type of officer desires to be feared, because as a child they may have been *"the frightened."* Although this is not a proven point, the research would make for interesting reading, but what officer would admit they were bullied as a kid. Some officers might reveal they were bullied as children desiring to feel like a hero to all those poor kids who are bullied today. Their intentions begin noble, but after a while, the cynicism that comes with the job may influence the bully within them. This type of officer is going to take care of the bad guys; they will go over and beyond to protect the citizens within the communities they patrol. These officers work the streets every day, and regardless of the situation, they give 100% to their duties and exude an air of confidence with a sense that they are in charge and they are the bully now.

We should not *fear* the police; they are supposed to be there to *help*, to protect and serve the community. Because of a history of racial disparity in black communities and recent incidents involving the killings of black citizens who were seized by police officers, some members of the public have exacerbated a rift between police and citizens. Both law enforcement officers and citizens have to work together to ensure we are clear on the function of police and how they perform their duties. This has to be accomplished in our most basic interactions. When I was a uniformed officer, I would occasionally encounter women with children who would stop me with their young toddlers in tow and say, "Look at that police officer. She is going to arrest you." I would immediately tell them not to do that because it creates a sense of fear in the child at an early age. What if the child finds him/herself in trouble? That one horrible encounter may discourage them from contacting the police, so please don't do this! Don't send a message that the sole function of the police is to arrest people. These type of negative interactions impact children for life. We must do better.

    The bottom line is a police officer is a human being, a neighbor, a spouse, a sibling, a parent, a student, a church member, a teammate. They are just like you. When you go to work, isn't it your goal to get home to your family afterward? Well, that is the same goal of every officer who wears a badge, and they will do what is necessary within the law (some outside the law) to make it home. Let's treat officers as they are, like us, until an officer gives you a reason to treat **them** (not all) differently. To both citizens and police: There MUST be a mutual respect for each other if for no other reason than the fact we are all human.

My purpose is not to make excuses for bad police officers or imply that race is not an issue in citizen/police encounters, but rather to help you understand the officers who commit to protecting and serving those within the communities that employ them. I do not speak for any particular officer, merely making generalizations based on my own experiences.

Whichever type officer responds to your "call for service" ensure that you are calm and can assist the officer in assisting you. Please understand that although these police officers should be there to help and your issue should be the priority, they are still human and endure the same human issues that you endure. If you have an issue with an officer, you always have the right to go to the next higher level and beyond to express your complaint.

3
COMMUNICATING

Rule 3: *Knowing how to communicate effectively with law enforcement personnel and 911 operators is important in obtaining the answers we seek. However, it is also important to know how to make valid complaints when we do not get the information we seek or treatment we deserve.*

Communication is accomplished, whether intended or not, in every action or non-action we are communicating. For communication to be effective a clear message must be given, and that same message has to be received, then there should be feedback from the receiver for the communication process to be complete. Citizens utilize an officer's verbal and non-verbal communication to determine their response and police officers utilize a citizen's verbal and non-verbal communication to determine their actions. Incidents that might result in an arrest may depend on the police officer who responds to that particular incident and their ability or inability to effectively communicate. An example might be an officer pulls a vehicle over for an inoperable brake light. As the officer approaches, he/she says in an angry tone, "You need to fix your brake light." This may be communicating that your brake light is inoperable; however, it does not **clearly** convey the message of why the officer pulled you over. If the citizen's response matches the angry tone of the officer in his/her demands to know why the officer pulled them over, the officer could then extend the traffic stop beyond the initial brake light infraction and imply that the operator of the vehicle was obstructing them from performing their duties or that the citizen was disorderly. While it is important that our police officers possess the ability to communicate effectively, citizens who encounter these officers should also be effective communicators.

There are two basic types of communication, verbal communication, and non-verbal communication. Police officers often utilize a person's non-verbal communication to plan their response. For example, an officer responds to a call for service regarding several people loitering outside a convenience store. When the officer arrives, he/she exits the vehicle and not wanting to implicate the store manager called the police, for safety reasons, he/she asks the people who were identified as loitering if there was a reason they were gathered outside the store. Immediately one of the people turns his baseball cap backward and begins to look around. An experienced officer knows the person who turned their cap to the back is probably looking for a path to flee. Suspects sometimes turn their baseball cap to the rear, so it does not blow away as they flee from the police. The actions of the citizen was totally nonverbal. The officer has to be aware of non-verbal communication just as much or even more than verbal communication. This is a reason officers often want to see your hands. As an officer, if I know what your hands are doing, they are less likely to hurt me.

Communication is necessary for maintaining a safe and secure environment. We communicate with our neighbors, with police, and with politicians. When you are a witness or a victim of crime you may have to communicate with a 911 operator. This chapter will prepare you with the questions you may be asked when calling 911.

Neighbors

Our neighborhoods are much different than those of the past, on every street, in every community everyone knew everyone. It was a time when "the village" truly raised the children. When someone went to a parent advising them, their child was involved in some bad behavior, what that person said had merit, and the bad behavior resulted in disciplinary action from the parent. Those days have passed and have been replaced with more transient living, where people move from residence to residence, multiple times. There are several factors that contribute to this moving, such as children having behavioral issues at school, the potential for increased rent at the end of a lease, environmental issues that impact the health and welfare of a family in addition to issues identifying viable transportation.

It is imperative that neighbors communicate. Local police departments suggest creating neighborhood watch programs. I suggest before setting up a neighborhood watch, know who is in your neighborhood. Get to know your neighbors. You can accomplish this by having a neighborhood meeting. This can be done anywhere, a local park, a church or a community center. I would suggest not using someone's home unless you are very familiar with everyone in the neighborhood. These meetings should be inclusive of everyone who lives in the neighborhood, and some people tend to be peculiar about who they allow inside their homes, as they should be. Well you say, we will be gathering in the back yard, there is no need for anyone to go into the house. Well, what if they have to use the restroom, just before an important segment. Are you going to send them home? No. So, again I suggest not having a meeting at your home until you are very familiar with **everyone** in the neighborhood. Burglars sometimes use these opportunities to surveil a home before committing a crime.

The very first meeting should consist of introducing yourselves. You will be surprised what you have in common with some of your neighbors. Use this first meeting to simply get to know each other a little. Save the stressing leadership choices until a next meeting. During the meeting discuss problems that have been noticed within the neighborhood. An issue that might be discussed in a neighborhood meeting might include sightings of strangers walking in the neighborhood. Neighbors also talk about incidents that involve crime, such as vehicle break-ins, burglaries, and vandalism. Before everyone leaves ensure there is a clear means of communicating the next meeting and addressing the issues that were brought up in the first meeting. Effective neighborhood associations are those that communicate regularly. Social media has allowed communities to keep in touch daily. A good example of a community utilizing social media was when a man who came home from work realized his home was burglarized. He immediately checked his surveillance camera footage and observed the criminals. He uploaded the video to the community page and before the next day someone identified one of the suspects. Without that clear video and the neighborhood social media page those criminals may have targeted a neighbor the next day. Because the neighbor identified one of the suspects, additional burglaries were prevented. The most important function of a neighborhood watch is to keep watch for everyone in the neighborhood.

Keep in mind everyone who comes to these meetings may not have the same goal—so, do not reveal issues with security around your home or vacation plans. For example, you would not want to tell anyone in an open meeting that you don't have an alarm or that your security cameras haven't worked in years. Those are things you should keep to yourself or only tell a close neighbor that you have a good relationship with, maybe someone who usually keeps an eye on your home when your family goes on vacation.

After the second or third meeting and the group has identified and decided on group leaders, a reliable means of communication has been implemented, and group policies/procedures have been discussed invite the police department to speak with your group. Most local agencies have community outreach programs that assist neighborhood watch organizations in their efforts to deter criminal activity. The officers assigned to these units act as a liaison between the community and the police department. They may come out and give your group information regarding crime statistics in your area and suggestions on how to combat the types of crime your community may be experiencing. Communication is the key! Neighborhood watches are a means to organize neighbors to be more proactive in deterring crime by providing organized communication. It is not a vigilante crime patrol. Your local police department can provide detailed information to keep your group organized and in compliance with local laws and ordinances.

Complaints

We often encounter police personnel in various places, such as the grocery store, neighborhood meetings or an officer may respond to our residence to gather information for a police report. When communication with police officers fail, whether it is an unclear message sent by either party or the failure of one or both parties to effectively understand the message received, it can create a negative encounter. The impact of a negative citizen/police encounter can leave an officer in a position in which they feel there needs to be some punishment for the citizen, i.e. citation or custodial arrest. The citizen can also feel there needs to be some punishment for the officer such as a complaint.

By the time a citizen has come to the conclusion they wish to make a complaint against an officer they will have expressed their displeasure and anger to many people other than police personnel. Examples of complaints include being stopped by an officer and being unhappy with the unprofessional manner in which you were treated along with the fact you received a citation. Rather than immediately going to the police department to file a formal complaint you contact everyone on your cellphone contact list to express your anger. Another example may be when an officer responds to your home for a burglar alarm and finds you present inside the home. The officer points their firearm in your face and tells you to get on the floor. In a rude tone, they then ask you for identification without explaining why. The actions of the officer and the unprofessional tone of questioning and unwillingness to explain their actions may have caused you to become angry. Rather than quell your anger and ensure that the officer's unprofessional behavior is addressed by completing a written complaint, you contact family and friends to complain about your treatment. Misery truly loves company; however, reasons people complain to friends and family may include seeking validity and empathy. They have a desire to make people feel what they felt and have them relate to the negative experience. The problem with complaining to our family and friends is our complaints almost never get addressed by the people who have the power to address them. How you make a complaint is just as important as the content of your complaint. Law enforcement agencies have made complaining about negative citizen/police encounters easier. They have equally made commending officers who go above and beyond the call of duty easier. Generally, agencies have some sort of online method of reporting a complaint or commendation. If a citizen does not have access to a computer, there may be a means to leave a recorded complaint by phone. Lastly, there is always the option to make the complaint in person.

There are certain things you want to remember when making a complaint about an officer to a law enforcement agency. First, ensure your complaint is valid. A valid complaint should address violations of policy/procedures, such as excessive use of force. A complaint can also be made if an officer is unprofessional or disrespectful by using vulgar language. Finally a complaint can be made if an officer violates of your rights afforded by the Constitution. The complaint should address the behavior of the officer and not necessarily a complaint about a citation you may have received. The fact of whether you were guilty of the offense or not should be addressed in court.

During my tenure as a beat officer, I found traffic stops were a catalyst to many citizen complaints. A complaint I most often had to address was signing a traffic citation. Citizens do not understand in some jurisdictions, the law requires you to sign a traffic citation. Generally, the bottom of the citation reads something like, "You are signing this citation in lieu of bond." This means you are being arrested by the officer for a traffic violation, but rather than taking you to jail (a custodial arrest) they are going to allow you to continue on your way with just your signature. In this instance, your signature acknowledges you are aware of your charge and the date you are to appear in court to answer to the charges. If an officer advises you, you must sign the citation or go to jail. That's not some unprofessional idle threat. The officer is simply following the law.

Second, make sure your complaint is organized. Unfortunately, police personnel may judge your complaint as valid or not by the way it reads. Take the time to write your complaint in an organized manner from beginning to end. Tell a story about what happened and include how the officer made you feel. Include all details, no matter how insignificant you think they may be. Always include your actions! If the officer approached you and used vulgar language and you responded by using vulgar language make certain you include your language in the complaint. When these complaints are investigated, the investigating officer is charged with finding the truth about what occurred. Their process will include contacting the officer and contacting you to ask questions about your complaint. After obtaining a statement from the officer, the investigator finds you omitted the fact that you used vulgar language in the encounter with the officer. When you omit **your** inappropriate behavior in a complaint, it gives the officer's version more validity.

Thirdly, ensure your complaint is grammatically correct. If you have difficulty spelling, writing, reading, etc. do not allow those deficiencies to prevent you from making a formal complaint. Find someone who can read, write, spell, etc. to assist you in writing your complaint.

Fourth, do not be rushed to leave your complaint with police personnel. Ensure you have obtained the name, rank badge number and position of the person you are giving your complaint to. Also, ask about the process, determine how long it will take until the next communication, who that communication will be with and a contact number for them. Ensure you follow up the next day with the person who took your complaint.

> **This really happened**: A citizen requested to make a complaint on an officer and asked for a complaint form. He was given a sheet of paper that had a line for name, address, date of birth, gender, time and a signature line, nothing special, just blank lines to write. The citizen was told he had to complete the complaint inside the police precinct. When he refused and attempted to take the form away from the precinct, the officer who gave him the form threatened to arrest him for theft if he left the precinct with the form.

There are some issues other than police behavior that a citizen may complain about. Again the issue is who to complain to. I watched a neighborhood go from a drug infested area with properties in disrepair to a model suburban neighborhood with manicured lawns in a span of approximately three years. How did this happen? Citizen involvement and complaints. People laugh when I say this, but it is totally true. The area I am referring to was a run-down area that had very cheap real estate. The cost to purchase property in this area was very inexpensive in comparison to other metro areas. The area was close to the airport and major interstates. One couple purchased a home, remodeled and moved in. It seemed like instantaneously beat officers were mandated to perform more patrols of the area. There were road safety checks that were conducted in the area. The police presence had been increased. But why? COMPLAINTS! This one couple began to complain about homeless people roaming the streets and living inside vacant homes in the area. They took these complaints not to the beat officer, but directly to the police chief and mayor. If you are complaining about the lack of officers patrolling your area, send an email to the chief, mayor, city council member, county commissioner or sheriff. I guarantee they will make certain that the complaint gets into the right hands. The old saying "crap rolls downhill" is true in this situation. The mayor, city council, county commission and sheriff are elected officials and would probably like to maintain a reputation that they are concerned with what happens in their respective areas. If your local representatives are not concerned about what occurs in your community and unreceptive to your complaints, use your *vote* to remove them. Although a police chief is not elected, sending a copy of your complaint to an elected official such as a mayor, city council member or county commissioner will usually garner results.

In complaining to elected officials and department heads such as a police chief, be respectful and informative. Give the police chief the benefit of the doubt that they are unaware of your concern. When communicating send a friendly, professional (no cursing and name calling) email or letter expressing the problem that you are experiencing and request a response within a certain period of time. *Do not make phone calls for complaints if possible!* Emails are great; you can always make an open records request for the response to those emails. If you do not receive a response, send a second email to the chief expressing that you understand they are busy and that this is the second attempt to reach her/him. Again, ensure the tone used in the email is professional. Send this second email to the mayor and your city council representative or county commissioner (if you do not live within the city limits), using the Cc line. Do not use Bcc (blind Cc). You want the chief to know you have included their supervisors for the second email. In your email, you should request a response in a certain period of time. When you have attempted to address your issues by sending an email, there is no doubt that you have attempted to communicate your issue, but do not stop there. Educate your neighbors about the issue and how the issue impacts them, then encourage them to send emails as well. It may be easy to ignore a single person, but it is very difficult to ignore an entire neighborhood. Be vocal and if you are not attending city council and county commission meetings, then start now. Know how your local government runs and who is there to represent your best interest and the interest of your community.

Most local governments include a time for citizens to make remarks during open meetings. These are opportunities to express your concerns to local government officials. Remember to be tactful and speak professionally.

> **Personal Anecdote:** *That reminds me of a situation I had while collecting for my paper route. I was fourteen-years-old at the time. We arrived at this residence, where we had left a newspaper every day for a month, and now it was time to pay the piper. From the time I began until that moment, this address was on my route. I knocked on the door, and a middle-aged man opened the door. I said good afternoon and introduced myself, at which time the man said, "I didn't get a paper." Before my dad could say anything, I said, "Yes, you did I threw it on your porch every day, and you owe me. If you don't pay, I will have to" as I held my hand out for the money. My dad explained to him that because I delivered the paper, we would have to pay for the month if he did not. The man left and returned with funds to cover the month. My dad waited until we got all the way home as we sat on the porch counting the money collected and updating our records. He then, out of the blue, said, "You don't have any tact." I was looking around the porch for some thumbtacks. He then explained what the word "tact" was. He was right I didn't have any, and some might say I still don't have any. I learned that day that it was easier to get things from people with honey (all sweet) rather than lemon juice (sour attitude).*

Complaints about lack of police patrols or officer presence are usually taken seriously, and the response may be to give you exactly what you want. Be prepared for the law enforcement agency's response. The beat officer may be asked to make additional documentation in reference to their patrol activities. A great means of documenting the officer was present in a certain location could be by issuing traffic citations. Before GPS equipped vehicles this was the standard means of documenting a request for additional patrols. You cannot doubt the officer was there when they have ten traffic citations for failure to stop at a stop sign. So, if this is your complaint make certain you and your neighbors are following the law. Although GPS equipped vehicles may not be monitored 24/7, agencies may have the ability to archive this information and retrieve it to refute or substantiate complaints involving patrol techniques. If there is documentation that the assigned officer has patrolled the area at some time during the shift you may be identified as a complainer by beat officers. To avoid this label make sure there is a significant issue that can be justified by concrete evidence such as recent burglaries, car break-ins or people loitering in the area and not just a belief that you "never" see a patrol vehicle in your neighborhood.

> **TIP:** Unless you are glued to your front window 24/7, there is no way to say with certainty that there is not an officer patrolling your neighborhood. It is impossible for an officer to be everywhere all the time.

Emailing the chief of police and local politicians should be used for significant issues in your community. I would not suggest knocking out an email every time you see a group of kids walking down the middle of the street talking loudly but if it becomes a nuisance and it is in violation of the law or local ordinance, by all means, make contact with the police department and ask for an incident report. If that process does not work then follow up with a supervisor. If that does not work follow up with the supervisor's supervisor and so on until your concern is addressed. That is how neighborhoods change.

Remember, if you are complaining, you have to tell everything you did and everything the officer did. If after writing it down you feel like your behavior was not so good either, then maybe you don't have a complaint, maybe we have to be more professional if the expectation is that we want the police to be more professional and vice versa. Please do not misunderstand me, NOTHING gives police officers the right to be disrespectful, but my Mom always told me that to get respect we have to give respect.

In the past, law enforcement was a very noble and respectful job, but now with technology and 24-hour news cycle, we see some police officers as not so perfect, not always so respectful. Does that mean citizens have to get on a lower level because the police might be on a low level? Also, what about those officers who are respectful? Everyone has bad days and generally when we are approached by the police we automatically believe it is going to be a bad day but it doesn't have to be that way. I challenge you to think positively when encountering the police it just might make the encounter and the outcome a little better.

Calling 911

Communicating with 911 operators can be a life or death event. When contacting 911 try to be calm and explain your emergency in detail. These operators have a very stressful job. For an entire shift, they listen to excited people who are in the midst of an emergency or observing someone else in the midst of an emergency. These operators are the first layer to receiving public safety assistance. When speaking with them, it is important to be calm especially if there is a language barrier or a strong foreign accent. These barriers can result in the operator having difficulty understanding the caller, which may result in the operator asking the caller to repeat details wasting valuable time. Speak slowly and give the operator details. Give detailed descriptions of the perpetrators and victims. Also, give details about injuries and how they occurred. Remember the operator is just the first layer. They have to take the information you provide and give that information to responding personnel whether the response is by fire personnel, police personnel or medical personnel.

The operator is trained to ask specific questions to assist them in getting you the response that is best suitable for your emergency. The first question may be what is the location of your emergency. This is so the operator can at the least know where the emergency is and get the appropriate personnel on the way. The next questions involve obtaining information about what is exactly happening; they will ask you to provide descriptions of any weapons used in addition to the number of victims and perpetrators.

When reporting criminal activity, it is necessary to provide a detailed description of perpetrators. These descriptions are integral in officers effectively investigating the call for service. When an officer is given a description, it is important that the description is detailed. For example, an officer is responding to an afternoon home burglary. The victim's home is in a racially diverse neighborhood. The caller describes the perpetrator as a white male, wearing a white t-shirt and blue jeans. Because school is not in session, there are groups of juveniles "hanging out" near the basketball courts, tennis courts, playground and the pool area. Some of these teens are white, and some are black, some are wearing jeans, and some are wearing white t-shirts. Because the description given to the officer was so vague, the perpetrator could be any of the people in the neighborhood or could be none of the people in the neighborhood. The goal when giving a description is to assist the officer in apprehending the perpetrator. The best means of accomplishing this goal is by providing a detailed description of the perpetrator. Taking the previous example, we give the following description: a white male, long blonde hair, blue baseball cap with a black five on the front, white t-shirt with a yellow smiley face on the front, blue jeans with holes in the knees and green gym shoes. There is a huge difference between this description and the first description given.

If a crime is being committed against you or someone else be calm and pay attention. It is just like in that movie about the abduction of a young girl. You have to be calm and pay attention to everything about the suspect such as how they look, what they are wearing, and how they speak. Do not leave to get your phone from another room because you might miss something. If your phone is near you by all means grab your phone. There is nothing better than video evidence of a crime. If there are multiple phones at the scene use one to call 911 and another to record the incident. When providing a description give it in detail from head to toe, knowing this ahead of time, you are more apt to pay attention to the perpetrator in an organized manner, thus obtaining the necessary descriptors. Ask yourself the following questions: What was their skin tone? (race cannot always adequately describe a person), What was their hair like? (straight, curly, short, long, afro, dreadlocks, braids, twists), What kind/color of hat or cap were they wearing? (knit cap, straw hat, baseball cap) Were their piercings or tattoos in their face? What kind/color shirt were they wearing? What kind/type of pants were they wearing? The shoes a perpetrator wears are very important because generally a smart criminal may think to change shirts, even pants but they rarely change shoes. Take note if they were wearing gym shoes or loafers in addition to their color. Was the suspect tall or short? Use your own height to determine their height. Were they taller or shorter than you? Were they obese or slim? Was there anything else significant about the suspect? Did they limp? Did they have an accent when they spoke? The more detailed you are when you call, the better chance the police have at stopping the actual suspect. It prevents police from wasting time stopping people who are not involved.

  Having a witness to the crime is great for the police but only if the witness is willing to be an active part of the investigation. Simply calling 911 is not the end of it. In this example, a police officer will not be able to arrest the suspect without a warrant unless they witnessed the burglary. Unless there is a witness who is willing to positively identify the perpetrator or there is some evidence that would clearly implicate the person who was stopped, the officer may be only able to obtain the personal information of the person stopped and provide that information to detectives for a follow-up. A witness who is willing to be involved would be taken to the location of the suspect, by an officer to conduct a "show up". The point of the "show up" is for the victim/witness to identify the perpetrator without the perpetrator knowing who is identifying them. The officer usually places the victim/witness in the rear of a patrol car, and they are driven to the suspect's location, but they are only driven close enough for the victim/witness to see the suspect and not so close that the suspect sees the victim/witness. The victim/witness is then asked if they see the person who committed the crime. The victim/witness should be told by the officer that the person stopped may or may not be the person who committed the crime. Generally the suspect is not placed into handcuffs; however, if they are do not let this influence your decision. Even if you provide the officers with a video or photo of the suspect, it does not mean they have stopped the correct person. They may have located someone who was dressed like the suspect or who looked like the suspect. The person who was stopped may also be seated with officers standing around them, but it does not necessarily mean they are guilty of anything other than being in the wrong place at the wrong time. When making suspect identifications, if you are not sure it is ok to say you are not sure. If the person stopped is not the person you saw do not try to convince yourself they are. If the officer has to release the person they stopped it does not mean the actual perpetrator will not be arrested it just means the case has to be forwarded to someone who can follow-up by conducting interviews and gathering evidence. Officers also have to realize if the arrest cannot be made based on witness information it is ok. It is better to utilize the information obtained and allow detectives to follow-up rather than arresting the wrong person.

Research shows eye witness accounts are the least reliable of any evidence obtained and it should be treated as such. There are several factors that influence a witness's ability to identify a perpetrator. Those factors include exposure time, delay in the time a witness observes the crime and the time they are asked to identify a suspect, the amount of attention they give to the suspects characteristics, weapon focus and outside influence.

The exposure time is the actual amount of time the witness is focused on the suspect. A witness who might observe someone kicking in the front door of a neighbor, but leaves to get a phone to contact police and misses the suspect exiting through the back door, would have only had a glimpse of the suspect and probably never saw the suspect's face. Depending on the amount of mental focus and attention they gave to that glimpse of the suspect, they may not be a very good candidate for a positive suspect identification. What they can provide is a building block to a positive identification. Maybe one neighbor observed the suspect kick the door, and they can give police a very accurate clothing description from the back. Maybe a neighbor on the next street sees the suspect leave the house through the back door carrying a large television and gives a clothing description from the front and back. In addition to those two witnesses, a third neighbor sees the suspect get into a blue vehicle with a large television and takes a mental note of the suspect's facial features in addition to his clothing and a partial tag number. All three of these witnesses together can create a picture of the suspect through the entire crime. Together they will provide a strong witness account that may result in a conviction; however standing alone at least one of them may not be enough to get a conviction.

    The delay in time from when a witness first observes a crime and suspect to when they are asked to identify the suspect can also be a factor in whether an identification is accurate. In general, officers conduct "field identifications" or "show-ups" within a reasonable time after the crime has occurred. After officers respond to the scene of a crime, they will check the area for suspects, based on the descriptions provided. If a suspect is not immediately located during that check of the area the reporting officer gathers the information for the report and provides the victim with a case number. The case is then referred to an investigator for follow-up. The officer who is responsible for patrolling that area usually keeps a look out for suspects matching the description given. Later that night an officer observes someone matching the description given earlier that day. Because there is too much time that has lapsed between the initial observance of the suspect and the time in which someone matching the description was located, the information is gathered and passed on to an investigator. The investigator then obtains a photograph of the suspect who was stopped along with 5 or more other photos. The investigator places those photos together, in what is called a photo array or a photo lineup. The photographs are usually similar to the suspect's photo. The investigator then goes back to the witness and reads them what is called an admonition statement. The statement explains the group of photos may or may not contain the person who committed the crime. The statement also explains the suspect you saw may have had a different hairstyle and could have grown facial hair. This is important to note so that witnesses are not looking for those features. Reviewing a photo lineup or a photo array requires that the witness pays close attention to facial features rather than hair styles and facial hair. Victims more than witnesses may be better at identifying suspects because of the time they may have had to focus on the suspect's features.

Weapon focus is very simple, the presence of any weapon demands a person's attention. When a crime occurs, and a person is faced with a weapon their attention turns to the weapon rather than the person holding the weapon. The weapon is generally described 'to be much larger than the actual weapon. Gathering a suspect description from these witnesses is a difficult task. Asking them to make a positive identification is also difficult because they try to fill in blanks with what they believe may have been identifying descriptors.

Lastly, outside influences can impact a witness identification. A crime may occur but prior to police arriving witnesses and a victim discuss what occurred and what the suspect looked like. The victim described the suspect as being a black male with dreadlocks wearing a blue t-shirt and green shorts. One witness who was very confident he saw the suspect as the crime was occurring described him as a black male with a short afro wearing a green t-shirt and blue jeans. A female witness stated they were both wrong and the suspect was a Latino male with short black hair, wearing a blue t-shirt and blue jeans. When the police arrived they separated the three people and placed them into three different rooms. The investigator spoke with the male witness who described the suspect as a black male with a short afro, wearing a blue t-shirt and blue jeans. The female witness described the suspect as a black male with short black hair wearing a blue t-shirt

> **TIP:** It is important to know an officer can detain someone based on a **BOLO** or **Be On Look Out**. This is called an investigatory stop. A BOLO is simply a description provided over a police radio from police officers to other police officers, or a written notice that includes a photo or description of the suspect.

and blue jeans. The victim described the suspect as a Latino male with short black hair, wearing a blue-t-shirt and blue jeans. The descriptions given to investigators by the victim and witnesses were different from the descriptions they provided to each other. The changes were based on their discussions and the lack of confidence in their own perceptions. Because the initial descriptions were so different, it is probable that someone was wrong but the investigator will not be able to easily determine that because the victims and witnesses were allowed to converse about the incident which influenced their individual accounts of the incident. This can pose a challenge to officers who are tasked with locating the perpetrator of a crime. This is why it is important for victims and/or witnesses to be separated to ensure the story they are telling is **their** story.

Police Officers

When communicating with a police officer remember what your parents said about getting more with honey than vinegar. These officers are sometimes under pressure, afraid, have issues outside of work, or they may just not like what they are doing for a living. It is not necessary to try to figure out what is going on with the officer just remain calm, speak slowly, take your hands out of

> Tip: Sarcasm is not an effective means of communicating.

your pockets, and don't make any sudden movements. We would like to think we know what we might expect from the police but their behavior is generally a response to the citizen's behavior. So I say again when dealing with the police remain *calm*! In most cases, if you were pulled over there was a reason. If you were stopped, there was a reason. Most officers will tell you why they stopped you or what they pulled you over for. Asking a citizen "Do you know why I stopped you?" is dialogue some officers will use to get you to admit guilt. If asked this question just politely say "No officer, I don't know. Why did you stop me?" When speaking to the officer do not have a negative or condescending attitude, but say it calmly and professionally, as if you really don't know. The main thing to remember is you don't want to give them any fuel for the fire. Remain calm!

Most officers have made up their mind whether you will receive a citation (a ticket) before they ever approach the vehicle.

Other officers base their decision on your responses. When I was a patrol officer, I had a certain speech. Generally, if I got my speech out without an interruption, I would give the violator a warning. If I was interrupted with things like, "I did stop at the stop sign," or "I didn't run that light," oh buddy, you were definitely getting a citation because the person is now, in essence, calling me a liar. I used my speech every time I pulled a car over. Here is what I would say for a morning pull over: *"Good morning ma'am/sir. The reason I stopped you is because you (insert violation). May I see your driver's license? (License is received). Thank you. I will be back with you in a moment."* I returned to my vehicle and used my computer to check whether the license was valid, vehicle registration was valid, vehicle insurance was valid, if there were any outstanding warrants on the driver, and if the vehicle was stolen or not. I then returned with either a citation, a verbal warning or written warning for the driver. Sometimes the end result depended on the driver's reaction to the situation, so ***stay calm!***

There are many different suggestions about how to act when pulled over by a police officer. I offer this suggestion, stay calm which generally places the officer at ease.

> TIP: If you have a situation in which you wish to have a police report written, make sure you make that clear to the officer before they leave. You have to be clear if you want a police report.

When encountering the police it is important to listen and perform the tasks the officer is requesting. I have been stopped by the police before, and I do not reach into my pockets in front of a police officer. If I need to retrieve my driver license, I do so as soon as I put my car in park, long before the officer approaches the vehicle. I refrain from doing a lot of movement as that too may cause officers to become alarmed. Generally, I do not identify myself as an officer when I am stopped because I do not want it to appear as if I am expecting some kind of favor from the officer. Although I keep a firearm on my person, I do not tell police officers that I am armed (there is no law requiring me to do so). As an officer, knowing that a person is armed always places me in a position of higher alert. Although I have never drawn my weapon because someone said they were armed, I have altered my behavior. Rather than returning to my vehicle to run a driver license during a traffic stop, I would remain outside the vehicle to run the license via radio. Knowing a driver or passenger was armed I would also request backup whereas in most cases I did not. Generally, only a law abiding citizen would acknowledge possession of a firearm because law abiding citizens want officers to feel comfortable.

Uses of force are often initiated because of a lack of compliance. In some of these incidents, there may be barriers to effective communication between the officer and the citizen. When the officer arrives, they have to establish order and then obtain the necessary information. Hands and the location of those hands are very important to officers. When encountering police, it is imperative that citizens listen and do what the officer says. If you have anything in your hands and the officer tells you to drop it, please drop it without hesitation. If the officer tells you to sit down, please sit down without hesitation. What people have to understand is that not all officers are the same. Some have the patience to allow citizens some leeway gaining compliance. Some officers are less patient and see a delay as obstruction. Some officers are afraid, and anything less than immediate compliance might be seen as aggression towards the officer. I believe when people are compliant police/citizen encounters are less likely to become negative. In any assault, the best witness is a victim. The victim must be alive to tell their story.

4
Police/Citizen Encounters

Rule 4: *There are only 3 types of citizen/police encounters. Knowing the requirements of each and how law enforcement officers move from one to the other can assist citizens with minimizing negative encounters.*

There are three recognized types of police/citizen encounters. Patrol officers, who regularly patrol assigned areas, are referred to as beat or patrol officers. Their job is to ensure their assigned areas of patrol are free from crime and when crime is identified they respond accordingly. There are proactive patrols in which the officer may drive a vehicle, ride a bicycle or walk to detect criminal activity. These officers, who citizens usually see riding or walking around their neighborhoods and shops, are generally mild mannered until a crime is committed or until they are challenged. Knowing this ahead of time can save you some drama when encountered by them. A police/citizen encounter can be initiated for a number of reasons. Law enforcement officers have a duty to protect us, but there is also a duty to serve the people. This service includes a number of activities such as assisting people to cross the street, providing directions, and helping with disabled vehicles. During my career I have assisted many people in doing a number of things. There are two that I will never forget and they both just happen to have been during a pouring rain. On a Sunday morning I was patrolling my area when a heavy rain began. It seemed like a monsoon. Seeing through the heavy rain had become difficult, but I could not help but see an elderly lady standing at a bus stop. She was standing without an umbrella not that it would have helped in a rain shower such as that one. I pulled my vehicle onto the sidewalk and exited with an umbrella and asked the lady if she would like a ride to her destination. I had no idea where she was going but it turned out she was on her way to church. I popped her in the backseat because the front was filled with equipment and drove her to church. The feeling I got when she turned to say thank you was unbelievable as I had not expected a thank you. I felt it was my duty to do it. I was just doing my job. There was nothing in the department policy that said I had to pick people up in the rain but I did because that is what good police officers do, serve the public. I see officers carrying groceries for elderly citizens and playing games with children; not a described duty of a police officer but it shows a connection with the people of the community. The second call I will never forget was a call for service involving a disabled vehicle on the interstate in the rain. Any call that an officer responds to on an interstate is a very dangerous call and has the potential to turn deadly, add the rain and it could go bad quickly. For some reason drivers are attracted to those pretty blue lights attached to police vehicles and have the propensity to run right into them. After locating the vehicle I met with a young man sitting inside a BMW who said he had a flat tire and wanted me to change it. He said he had never changed a tire and did not know how to get it done. I told him that although I would not be changing a tire for a man I would remain and walk him through changing the tire. My father taught me to check the oil in a vehicle and change a tire in addition to how to perform other preventive maintenance on a vehicle. I was surprised that this adult man did not know how to change a tire. I had him retrieve his tools from his vehicle but he did not know where to look. Eventually he located the tools and changed the tire. He was most appreciative that he had learned something valuable that day. This was truly an attest to my favorite quote *"Give a man a fish he will eat for a day, teach a man to fish and he will eat for a lifetime"* (Unknown). Most officers turn to a career of law enforcement with the goal to help make the world a better place but at some point departmental politics and cynicism change their attitudes and thus change the activities and behaviors of otherwise good officers.

The three levels of police/citizen interactions are consensual, investigative detentions, and arrests. That is it, only those three. When you know what type of encounter you are having it tends to help make it a bit more positive. Know where you fit in! There is usually no invite to the next level. An officer can go from one to another without you realizing it.

The Fourth Amendment to the US Constitution covers the right to be secure in your persons, houses, papers and effects against unreasonable search and seizure: *"This shall not be violated and no warrants shall be issued, but upon **probable cause**, supported by Oath or affirmation and particularly describing the place to be searched and the persons or things to be seized."* What this means basically is that the police cannot arrest you or search you or your things or home without **probable cause or a warrant**. *But* there are exceptions!

Consensual Police Encounter

A consensual encounter is one in which the citizen has to give consent for the encounter to continue. These encounters are used as fact gathering events to build a case against someone. This encounter is that friendly type of interaction that you have when you see an officer in the grocery store in which they may say hello or you may say hello. Another example is if an officer is on patrol, driving down your street, and they stop and say hello. Or you may by chance go into a police precinct to obtain information. When I was a beat officer I always began my citizen encounters by greeting the person with "Hello ma'am/sir, may I speak with you for a minute?", then I would introduce myself and begin with light small talk before I got to the reason I stopped them. If they said something like "Do I have a choice?" I would explain to them they did have a choice but what I had to ask would not take long. Usually they would stay and talk. Officers who are dishonest with the public in this instance could believe that deception and heavy handed tactics will get them farther than honesty. People generally want to believe police officers can be trusted and want to believe what they are told by police officers is the truth. In any type of relationship when trust is broken it generally takes a great deal of time and effort to regain that trust. Take a marriage for example. When you trust your partner and at some point learn that you have been deceived the trust is broken. It seems once you lose trust in your spouse it would be very difficult to get that trust back, without hard work. The same can be said for relationships between citizens and law enforcement. When citizens lose trust in police officers it is difficult to develop that trust again without sincerity and significant work. Even though all police officers are not the same, some citizens consider distrust of one officer as distrust for all officers.

The culture of the department sets the tone for what is acceptable and what is not. It dictates the departmental policies and procedures. It impacts what type of person is recruited and ultimately hired. There are departments that have a community involvement culture and those that have more of a superiority culture. There are also those departments that have a hybrid culture where their actions are dictated by the community they are serving. Departments that have a community involvement culture tend to have more community outreach programs that bring the officers and community members together to promote positive relationships. Their department's statistics may include a category related to citizen contacts. Those departments that have the superiority culture may tend to have fewer community outreach programs and rather than statistics involving citizen contacts they may only record arrests and traffic citations. The culture of the police department also impacts the decisions officers make related to who to stop and why to stop them. If stopping a black male standing on a corner doing nothing simply because he is wearing sagging jeans and a white t-shirt is acceptable behavior in that department then the behavior will be expected from officers within that department.

Racial profiling is a hot button issue in Black and Latino communities. "Racial profiling occurs when a person's race, ethnicity, religion or national origin is the determining factor in whether they will be stopped by police" (www.nij.gov). These stops are due to the stereotypical beliefs of officers and the acceptable culture of the department. For example, a black male who is standing on a corner, wearing sagging jeans and a white t-shirt could be stereotyped as someone who was involved in drug sales. The male was stopped for suspicion of selling drugs although there was no behavior that would provoke such a suspicion. There was no reasonable articulable suspicion that drugs were being sold, no complaint of drugs being sold and no probable cause drugs were being sold. The stop was only based on the race and description of the male. Profiling is an effective means of identifying criminal activity but such profiling is not and should not be based on race but rather a persons' behavior. In the above mentioned example, if the male was seen handing someone something and then receiving something in return in what is referred to as a "hand to hand transaction" an officer can articulate, based on their knowledge and training, that the behavior is often used in drug transactions. With that observed behavior, the man can now be stopped for an investigation based on the suspicion of selling drugs. There is a difference in racial profiling and profiling based on behaviors.

Although the three levels of police/citizen encounters are distinct, officers often go from one to the other without pause. It is important to know during a consensual encounter you have to give consent for the officer to continue the encounter. Officers are often able to transition from a consensual encounter to an investigative detention very quickly which is why it is important to know what questions to ask to ensure you are free to leave.

Things you should know when interacting with police include: Is this a consensual stop? Am I free to leave? Is there probable cause that requires me to stay here? Am I suspected of criminal activity? If so, what? These are all questions that an officer should provide answers to when asked. However, some officers who are less than secure in their knowledge of the law tend to utilize force and sarcasm, rather than reason, in these instances. They tend to "throw the weight of their badge around", ignoring the rules of engagement which include our Constitutional Rights.

In some jurisdictions, there are only certain instances in which you are required to show an officer your identification. The first instance is while you are operating a motor vehicle and the second is if you are suspected of loitering and prowling. The traffic stop is a no brainer. The officer has to ensure you are a licensed driver and the only way to adequately do that is to see your license. If you are stopped for loitering and prowling the officer has an obligation to investigate and dispel any suspicions that anyone may have about you being in a certain area. Part of the investigation is to determine who you are. Seeing an identification is an effective means of doing so.

During a consensual encounter, the officer can ask you anything they want, including, a popular question "Do you have anything on you I need to know about?" This is a very vague question and can lead a person to incriminate themselves. First of all, the person being stopped has to determine exactly what the officer means by "something I need to know about". The officer could be referring to a weapon that could be used against them or illegal narcotics. It could be a check that was written on a closed account. The point is they could be asking about anything. In this instance you have the Fifth Amendment Right against self-incrimination. During these consensual encounters what you say can and will be used against you. Another question is "Can I search you for illegal narcotics or weapons?" It is legal to ask this question and you have the right to refuse the request. This is a Fourth Amendment Right guaranteed by the United States Constitution. If you consent to the search, giving the officer permission to search you, whatever is found can and will be used against you. They can ask you if you committed a specific crime? Again, you have the Fifth Amendment Right against self-incrimination. If you answer yes to this question indicating you did commit a specific crime then you have provided the police with an admission of guilt. The means in which the admission was obtained would be perfectly legal because you initially agreed to speak with the officer. Any answer to this question other than no may encourage the officer to continue to dig for their answer.

Remember when interacting with police it is important to use tact. In some jurisdictions, they still have that unspoken law called "POP" (Pissing Off the Police). This unspoken law is usually disguised as an obstruction or disorderly conduct charge. What this means is some officers create a charge of obstruction and (or) disorderly conduct because they have been embarrassed or have become angry at the situation. Citizen behaviors that trigger this response from officers include asking questions related to why they are being stopped, cursing at them (which is not unlawful in most jurisdictions unless children are present), expressing the stop was unlawful and (or) an unjust use of force. So remember, use tact—there is no need to cause a scene and curse, stay calm. Officers are trained to watch the hands of people they stop. When people talk with their hands some officers may see this as aggressive actions and thus their response may rise to one of more aggressive nature. You must understand if the officer is asking for permission to speak with you and you do not wish to speak, you can look them in the eye and quietly say, "I do not wish to speak at this time. Have a good day officer." Unfortunately, sometimes our responses are the very thing that can escalate any interaction with police into a negative one. Even though you have the right to walk away from a police officer, in some instances, determining what it is the officer wants may be the best thing to do. If the officer cannot provide a reason for stopping you, you might say, "I do not wish to speak with you at this time." There is no need to be boisterous, belligerent, or cause a scene. You have the right to remain silent. Stay calm! The bottom line is with a consensual stop you have to give your consent.

In today's society the burden of proof of what we do is on us; which means unless there is **proof** something happened it didn't happen. Without some type of evidence that shows an officer was in violation of the law or policy judges and police administrators may tend to believe the version of the incident that the officer reports. It boils down to the citizen's word against the officer's word. In a perfect society we would like to believe the officers who are hired to protect and serve the citizens of the country are honest and with integrity. However, this isn't a perfect society. Although the law says you are innocent until proven guilty, in some instances, you might be guilty until proven innocent. If you think you are going to be stopped discreetly record the encounter or have someone else discreetly record it and ask questions. Ask "Is this a consensual encounter or am I being detained?" "What is the reason for the stop?"

When I was working in the field, either as a patrol officer or detective and I saw someone I wanted to speak with, but really didn't have a reason to stop them, I would ask, "Hey, can I speak with you for a minute?" Most people would stop and talk. Some would not. No sweat if they didn't want to talk. I would try again later or the next day. There is no reason for an officer to be rude and insist that someone stop and speak with them. An officer also should not insist upon someone stopping to speak with them unless the officer has articulable reasonable suspicion or probable cause.

Investigative Detention

The investigative detention is one step up from the consensual stop but not to the level of an arrest. The investigative stop is also used to gather information. The officer has to have at least articulable reasonable suspicion that a crime has occurred and that the person being stopped is related to the crime in some manner. What this means is that the officer must believe the person being stopped has committed, is committing, or is about to commit a specific crime. It has to be based on facts and observations that the officer can effectively describe as being criminal behavior based on their training and experience. Stopping a person based on a BOLO is a good reason to make an investigative detention provided the person you have stopped actually looks like the photo in a BOLO. A lookout over a police radio, which includes a good description, is another good reason for an investigative detention. Let's say, for example, a patrol officer is standing in line at a bank when she looks out the window and sees a guy across the street sitting inside a car with a ski mask on. There are no other buildings in the immediate area, the temperature is 70 degrees and it is not Halloween. I would say that guy's behavior (sitting outside a bank) and his description (wearing a ski mask) are indicative of a bank robber. This would be a good investigative detention. An officer can apply this to any crime. It is all about the behaviors, not necessarily about the person, their race, their ethnicity, or their location by itself, but a combination of things such as their behavior and location. In some cases, this is where you get your accusations of racial profiling. Simply being black in a predominately white neighborhood or being white in a predominately black neighborhood is not enough for an investigative stop. However, depending on the jurisdiction this justification of a stop may be a common practice although very wrong.

During an investigative stop an officer can search your **outer garments for weapons** if, and only if, there is reasonable suspicion that you might be armed. For example, let's say you match the description of a suspect that just committed an armed robbery at a bank around the corner. The officer has what is called *articulable reasonable suspicion* that you might be armed and can search your outer garments for weapons because the robbery was committed with a weapon. **Articulable reasonable suspicion** *is something only a law enforcement officer can have. It means based on their knowledge, experience, and training, they can describe the behavior being displayed as criminal behavior.* If you matched the description of a suspect who picked someone's pocket then the police do not have articulable reasonable suspicion that you might be armed because picking someone's pocket does not require a weapon. Thus, they should not be searching your outer garments for a weapon. This is not a consensual stop but an officer may ask you if they can search you for weapons which makes the search consensual. You have the right to say no if they ask for your permission to search you. You have to make it clear that you do not wish to be searched. Some officers ask to search in different ways so you have to listen to what they are asking so that you can provide the right answer. An officer can ask you, "Can I search you for weapons for my safety?" The proper response to deny them permission would be, "No". An officer asks, "Do you mind if I search you for weapons for my safety?" The answer here should be, "Yes", to deny permission. Regardless of how the question is asked make certain if you do not want to be searched your answer is clear and that you clearly express, "No, I do not want to be searched."

Some officers approach citizens and ask if they can conduct a search of the citizen's pockets *"to see if you have anything on you, "*. Again, if the officer **asks for permission** to search, you have the right to say no.

There are many exceptions to searching **a person** and you should know these exceptions. Three that could be important in an investigative or consensual stop include:

- **Consent-** You give the officer consent to search you
- **Plain view-**If an officer sees evidence of a crime without manipulating something to see it, it is considered to be in plain view.
- **Plain feel-**If during a pat down of the outer garments for weapons an officer feels what they

immediately identify as evidence of a crime they can remove that item and arrest you for possession of it.

All of your constitutional rights apply during any detention. It is important to know an investigative detention can lead to an arrest quickly. Now again, I'm no lawyer, and I am not offering you legal advice. Do your own research, know what your rights are, know what the police have the right to do, and know what they don't have the right or authority to do.

Arrest

It is important to know your state law as it relates to the age of an adult for arrest purposes. In Georgia, at the time this book was written the legal age to arrest someone as an adult is 17 years of age, but there are exceptions.

An arrest can only be made with **probable cause or an arrest warrant!** In some states a person is considered under arrest when their liberty to come and go as they please is restrained no matter how slight that restraint may be. This definition may or may not apply to you depending on the state you are in. It is important that you know the law where you are because laws and definitions vary from state to state, from city to city, from parish to parish and so on.

Based on the definition of arrest, perception is important. If a person is placed in handcuffs it is obvious they are not free to leave. If a person is surrounded by officers it is obvious they are not free to leave. On the surface both of these examples indicate a person has been arrested; however, officers and departments utilize an excuse of detainment to justify these actions. An officer should have at least articulable reasonable suspicion that the person being detained was involved in a crime. It should be noted that whether a person is detained or arrested they still have the right to remain silent.

There are two categories of crimes: misdemeanor and felony. Generally, city and county ordinances are considered misdemeanors. A misdemeanor is a crime that is minimal in nature compared to a felony but greater than an infraction of the law. An adequate comparison would be theft is to a misdemeanor as a seatbelt violation is to an infraction. Misdemeanors can be punishable for less than one year but not more than one year. A felony is a crime that can be punishable for more than one year. An example of a felony is murder. In some jurisdictions there are degrees and levels of felonies and misdemeanors such as class A felony, class A misdemeanor and class B misdemeanors and felonies. These designations are used to differentiate the seriousness of a crime. Some jurisdictions, like Georgia, use descriptive wording such as "misdemeanor of a high and aggravated nature" to differentiate the seriousness of a crime rather than utilizing a level or degree. These levels, degrees and descriptive wording can also indicate a difference in fines or punishment. Although you may be charged with a misdemeanor, a misdemeanor of high and aggravated nature or a class A misdemeanor can carry a maximum fine and jail time, whereas a Class B misdemeanor would be a lesser fine/punishment.

A police officer can make an arrest with an arrest warrant or without (warrantless arrest). When an officer obtains an arrest warrant a judge has heard sworn testimony and determined there was probable cause to make a lawful arrest. An arrest warrant can be served by any officer provided the warrant notice was entered on the National Crime Information Center (NCIC). Whether you will be arrested depends on the crime and the distance the jurisdiction is willing to travel to pick you up. For example, if you committed a burglary in Miami, Florida and moved to Seattle Washington, it is unlikely that Miami will extradite (come and pick you up). However, if given the same two cities, you commit a murder it is probable that Miami will extradite.

Requirements for a warrantless arrest include an officer being a witness to a crime and evidence of probable cause. The crime doesn't necessarily have to be committed in front of the arresting officer. The crime could have been committed in front of any officer who notifies other officers that the crime was committed in their presence along with the identity of the perpetrator or a detailed description of the perpetrator. Consult your states laws to determine when an officer can legally make an arrest in your state.

> **TIP:** Police officers are not obligated to provide information to parents of adult children who have been arrested.

Police Use of Force

Police officers have a great deal of responsibility and authority. In what other career does someone have the ability, opportunity and discretion to incarcerate someone or to take someone's life? None, that I can think of. Police officers are tasked with being psychologists, mentors, counselors and educators with no "formal" education to do so. They make decisions regularly that can dictate the future of entire families. This job requires a person who is capable and willing to not only put their life on the line for a total stranger, but to think. To cognitively assess each situation on its own merit and determine a viable outcome for all parties involved. A college degree does not necessarily guarantee this characteristic, but agencies encourage the recruitment of people with college degrees by offering them higher starting salaries.

The ideal police officer should be one who can think on their feet, not just tactically but cognitively and strategically to anticipate the consequences of their actions ahead of time. This can only come with quality training from a knowledgeable, experienced training officer with specific experience in providing good productive police services. The well-known mantra among law enforcement officers, "I would rather be judged by 12 than carried by 6" cannot and should not be the standard used in determining whether to use deadly force or not, although to this point the mantra has proven successful for the majority of those officers who were involved in deadly uses of force. The number of law enforcement officers in this country is vast and does not compare to the number of officers involved in deadly uses of force.

During the course of my career I have often wondered why some officers would not wait on backup, especially when approaching suspicious people. There were certain officers who, when they acknowledged they were responding to some calls for service, the supervisor already knew there was going to be force used in an arrest. These officers were not good at communicating with citizens, which is why it is always good to have a second officer present. The backup officer cannot simply be an enclosed fire alarm, there to be broken in case of an emergency. They have to be engaged and have enough courage to step in when things get out of hand or head down an unprofessional path. The "thin blue line" sometimes prevents backup officers from interfering during a call for service for fear of being identified as some sort of traitor and treated as an outcast. In some instances some officers are unable to address conflict by any means other than arrest. Although supervisors may be aware of the excessive uses of force during arrests, it can sometimes be said the officer was in an environment in which an arrest needed to be made. This mentality is not a result of racial prejudice but of a police culture in some departments that exacerbates an us versus them mentality. The officers I have referred to can be black, white, Latino and (or) Asian. Regardless of the officer's race or ethnicity they generally have a disdain for criminal activity which may be common in communities with a low socioeconomic status. Some officers may believe the residents in such a community are not worthy of respect and they are unable to understand if an officer speaks to them respectfully. I have had many officers say to me "They don't understand sir and ma'am you have to curse at them for them to understand what you are saying." This was not true in my experiences. I treated people with respect and I received respect in return. Those officers had the mentality that a few people in such communities represented the entire community. This is why it is important to understand the officer you have come into contact with. All police officers are not the same. The number of good community-oriented police officers far outnumber the officers lacking that attribute.

I found a great example of a culture of police officers who believed a group represented the whole. I was reading *"Cop in the Hood"* by Peter Moskos, who indicated a black officer commented "it's hard not to think that this is a jungle", referring to a predominately black and poverty stricken area of Baltimore. It was said the officer referred to the area as a jungle because of "people running around the street getting high and acting a fool" (Markos, 2008). Does that mean affluent neighborhoods or addresses in which the homes are well manicured are jungles as well? Even though drugs are known to be used in some of these homes and police are called to these homes to restore order just as in other communities; we do not associate these well-manicured homes with such activities. We unfairly associate them with professional, well-behaved people.

When I was in the field training program a senior officer always referred to a specific apartment complex as "Jungle Foot". I never asked why he called it that because I was sure it was something derogatory. The apartment complex was in drastic need of repair. There were broken windows held together by tape. The parking lot, the portion that was paved, had huge potholes and the rest of it was dirt which created some pretty large mud holes during a good rain. The majority of the residents were Latino and there were a sprinkle of white and black residents as well. Although this officer was a white male and didn't seem very fond of African Americans and Latinos he also had a disdain for poor white people. He referred to them as "six toes" and said it meant they were all born from incest. He spoke to them just as harshly as he did poor African Americans and Latinos. This guy had such a disdain for poor people but he always wanted to work in the poorer communities. It was because he too had a mentality that these people did not garner the respect that more educated citizens demanded. There was one beat (patrol area) that was filled with middle class and affluent African Americans to which this officer was assigned occasionally, causing him to feel he was being punished. In this area he had to be respectful to black folks or endure written complaints. My point is that officers sometimes but should not judge people by the location of their address, their socio-economic status, race, gender, nationality, religion or sexual orientation. Police officers should apply the law in a just manner. Everyone should be treated with respect. If the residents of those well-manicured homes can be treated with respect so should someone who lives in a crowded run-down apartment.

    There are many factors that can impact the decision of an officer to engage in a use of force. After becoming a supervisor I found officers who were aggressive and involved in repeated uses of force had difficulty communicating with the public. Their approach was always aggressive regardless of the incident. The manner in which they spoke to people was demeaning. It is difficult to alter the approach of these type officers by mentoring and training. They generally require progressive discipline with extensive documentation. The attitude of the officer and their inability to communicate effectively can create a barrier to effective communication. Barriers created by ineffective communication can lead to force being used against a citizen for minor infractions.

The unwillingness of a citizen to comply with the commands of an officer may often result in force being used. An officer is taught to take control of a scene upon their arrival. If people are arguing officers command them to stop arguing. If people are fighting officers command them to stop fighting. If people are fleeing officers command them to stop fleeing. If people are holding items in their hands the officer commands them to drop the items. Officers might command citizens to sit down to gain control of a situation. When these commands are not followed the officer may use force to gain compliance. Whether the officer is in compliance of department policies and the law when applying force depends on the "totality of the circumstances" which means everything that has occurred, background of the citizen involved, information victims/witnesses provided, environment, etc.

Mental health disabilities can also be a barrier that may cause officers to use force. The inability to understand and effectively communicate with someone with a mental health disability may lead an officer to believe force is the only manner to gain compliance. The fear that a person with a mental health disability will utilize some enhanced strength to cause harm to the officer may prevent effective communication with a citizen. There are certain mental health conditions in which people can become aggressive when someone enters their personal space, or touches them or prevents them from performing stress relieving techniques. For example, some autistic people have coping mechanisms that assist them when a mental crisis occurs such as shaking their hands and arms or pacing. An officer who is unaware of these types of coping mechanisms can exacerbate an encounter with an autistic person by not allowing them to utilize those coping mechanisms. Relevant, effective and ongoing training focused on providing police officers with the tools necessary to identify and assist people who may be having a mental health crisis is critical to decrease use of force incidents.

Negative attitudes of citizens can also impact a police/citizen encounter. Recent police involved shootings that have resulted in the deaths of citizens have created a negative perception of police officers. Those negative perceptions can promote a negative attitude and an unwillingness to effectively communicate and comply with a police officer's commands. This barrier like the others may cause the officer to use force to gain compliance. It should be noted all police officers are not the same. While there are some disrespectful, unprofessional officers there are also some officers who are approachable, professional and in the profession to help all people. There are unprofessional African American officers, Caucasian officers, Latino officers, Asian officers, etc. Please do not assume all police officers are the same simply because we wear the same type uniform. If you are angered by a police officer because you feel that you were treated unprofessionally use your pen to express that anger but always comply to lawful commands the officer may give.

The negative perceptions and oftentimes unprovoked killings of law enforcement officers have taken a toll on the law enforcement community and may have caused officers to be hyper-vigilant in carrying out their duties. An officer who may have never placed his/her hand on their firearm during a traffic stop may now do so. Officers who were reluctant to request backup may now do so more expediently. Officers who would use physical tactics to defend themselves in the past may resort to using non-lethal and lethal methods. Police officers generally use a defense of being in fear of their lives when using lethal force. I have spoken with some officers who are in fear before they are even faced with a decision of using lethal force. They are fearful they will be injured, unable to continue the career they have enjoyed or killed and unable to go home to their loved ones. This is often what is expressed by officers in Grand Jury and/or trial proceedings and for some jurors it may be difficult to hear that someone who put their life on the line for perfect strangers was fearful as they decided whether to take the life of someone else or for their own to be taken. The perceptions of citizens and attitudes or the fear that some officers feel when performing their duties is no excuse for unjustified use of deadly force. Those people who were killed as a result of deadly force encounters with police officers may have had fear as well. Fear that their actions when interacting with law enforcement officers may result in their death or serious bodily injury. These deadly use of force incidents have resulted in millions of dollars in civil penalties for various jurisdictions. Police departments cannot continue with business as usual. There must be significant steps taken to deter the "shoot first" mentality that some officers harbor. The public also has to be educated about police/citizen interactions and the importance of compliance. Citizens and police officers alike wish to walk away from every police/citizen encounter.

    The decision to use force, especially deadly force, should be one that requires the use of critical thinking skills. A well trained officer rehearses potentially dangerous encounters and utilizes critical thinking skills to determine the best response to those situations. It is important to critically think about potentially dangerous situations, analyze each possible response and determine the best response prior to being placed in that type of situation. No officer will face "every" possible potentially dangerous encounter but should anticipate worst case scenarios. Those negative encounters that arise from less than positive interactions with citizens can be minimized by using effective communication skills.

Police agencies are not alone in recruiting employees who are deficient in critical thinking skills. There are career paths in which this skill may not be as noticeable; however in law enforcement critical thinking skills are quite necessary. It is necessary to know the proper actions to take and how those actions will impact all involved. Because of this paradigm change officers require much more training than before. State mandates for training such as use of force and crisis intervention training attempt to ensure officers are equipped with the tools necessary to address issues involving force and mental illness in the field. However, there are certain factors that a department must address which can sometimes prevent officers from obtaining ongoing relevant training, such as an adequate number of available officers on duty, the quality of the training provided and the cost of such training. Law enforcement has experienced a number of changes since the 1950's and 1960's when police officers could do whatever they wanted without being called out for their actions. Although some may feel there hasn't been a change I would have to disagree with them. There are more people who are aware of the rights they have when interacting with police, there are more law enforcement agencies that utilize community policing strategies, there are more minorities who are employed as law enforcement officers within police agencies, there are more video surveillance systems in public areas and there is more technology that allows citizens to record officer's actions, all of which has influenced a significant change in law enforcement agencies across the country. Citizen created video recordings of police/citizen encounters have proven to be a great window into the activities of law enforcement officers, in addition to providing evidence of wrongdoing. Although those videos provide a wealth of information and enlightenment, rarely are the videos a complete narrative of an entire police/citizen encounter. Unless the video camera is rolling prior to the officer encountering a citizen there will always be important pieces missing thus allowing each side to fill in the blanks as they perceived the encounter. Generally, the beginning of the encounter is the most important because it may identify the probable cause for a stop. A video that begins after the officer beings to chase or strikes a citizen generally misses the probable cause the officer may have used to justify the stop, in addition to the justification for a use of force. The bottom line is video and audio recordings of police actions are very important and necessary in providing some visual narrative of police actions. However, they rarely provide all of the necessary information. Without video, in these cases, we are left with eyewitness testimony which can oftentimes be misleading. In my duties as an investigator I often interviewed witnesses of incidents who claimed to have seen criminal activity with their own eyes. In some cases, witnesses never saw anything but were influenced by others. I often encountered witnesses who heard things but reported they saw them instead. The mind will sometimes fill in the blanks for us in these instances. For example a robbery occurs at a store and the suspect shoots a clerk. A witness is across the street and hears the gunshot. They see a person run from the store. They believed they witnessed the robbery. In reality they only heard a gunshot and observed someone run from the store. It turned out the person running from the store was a customer who was inside and was now fleeing the shooter. Although the witness across the street heard a gunshot and saw someone running they didn't witness the incident. Based on the scenario the witness can only identify another witness. These mistakes happen often which is why it is important to have an experienced officer on scene who will utilize other witnesses, videos and evidence to corroborate every story.

5
POLICE TRAINING

Rule 5: *Knowing the requirements for employment, how police officers train and what training is required can help citizens understand the actions of law enforcement officers.*

Law Enforcement training is the cornerstone of the American Policing model. The needs of society dictate the philosophy of policing and as the policing philosophy changes the type and amount of required police officer training changes. This was evident from the August Vollmer era when the first "police school" was implemented. They utilized college educated professors and police officers to teach in areas such as police methods and procedures, first aid, public health, sanitation and criminal law to name a few. Vollmer's police school curriculum increased from one year to three years. The innovative policies that Vollmer implemented garnered him national notoriety and appreciation (Peak,2006).

As the philosophy in the Vollmer Era changed from a community involved model of policing in which officers were encouraged to address social aspects of the community and not simply focus on arrests of criminals, to a model based on crime fighting, the goals of training changed. There was no longer a need to train police officers in areas that involved social work and community involvement. In 1951, LAPD Chief of Police William Parker changed the way his officers were trained. They were required to endure thirteen weeks of rigorous physical and academic training in a recruit training academy. This model of training was shared and implemented by police agencies throughout the country. Parker's policies and philosophy were of a "law and order" mentality that was based on the belief that there were real threats to public safety and only a strong, aggressive police force was the answer. Parker's failure to gain public support for his policies coupled with an era of unrest due to riots, demonstrations, racial conflict and political fallout from the Vietnam war led to yet another change in philosophy (Peak, 2006).

After the **President's Crime Commission Report** was completed American policing returned to a policing model that was more centered on community involvement. Other changes that were implemented as a result of the report were increased minority hiring and building a more educated force through recruitment. Through both, the Reagan and Clinton Presidencies America saw a return to the "law and order" philosophy that included the "war on drugs." This fight against drugs caused police departments to implement strategies to control the drug activity and the crime this activity left in its path. There was increased use of specialized narcotics units to aggressively patrol the streets to combat drug crime. The Federal Government provided training and equipment to ensure the police were able to maintain the frontlines of this war on drugs. The aggressive patrols and investigative tactics used by these specialized narcotics units caused fractures in the relationship between police and the communities they served. This fracture resulted in a call for a change in the methods used to police the streets of America. In 1994, under the Clinton Administration, the policing model changed back to community oriented policing. Federal funding was used to ensure local agencies had the resources necessary to hire and train officers in community oriented policing strategies. These officers were expected to utilize their training to increase community involvement and promote partnerships with police departments and community members.

Recently, police involved shootings have increased demands from Americans for additional police training and reform of current policies related to deadly use of force and de-escalation. As stakeholders work through means to accomplish these tasks, it is important to understand how a police officer is hired, trained and the barriers that may prevent adequate ongoing training.

Over the years "law enforcement" has grown to include sheriff deputies, marshals, correction officers, parole officers and probation officers, however, in this section, we will be discussing police officer hiring and training. The application process for a police officer varies depending on the department applied to and the state the department is located.

Police training encompasses multiple levels of learning including the basic training received as a police recruit. Upon successfully completing requirements to obtain certification, officers are then placed with an experienced officer for additional training and guidance while responding to real world incidents. Throughout an officer's career, there are opportunities to participate in professional development classes that enhance, refresh and build upon the knowledge, skills, and abilities learned in basic training. There is also specialized training that provides an officer with advanced training in specific areas such as explosives, investigations, etc. Although training can be a viable solution to a number of issues surrounding law enforcement, the means to obtain that training can make such a simple solution very elusive. This chapter will discuss the application process, police training, the importance of ongoing relevant training and what can be done to improve the facilitation of training.

Application Process

Each state varies in the requirements, methods, quantity, and quality of basic law enforcement training. A very glaring difference is in New York Police Department (NYPD) and Atlanta, Georgia Police Department (APD). The NYPD allows a candidate to begin the application process at 17 ½ years of age; however, they must be 21 years of age by the time of hire. The applicant is also required to have 60 hours of college credit with a grade point average of 2.0 from an accredited college or university or two years of honorable military service. The APD requires an applicant be 20 ½ years of age. An applicant is not required to possess college credits but must have a high school diploma or GED. Los Angeles Police Department (LAPD) is similar to APD as they require an applicant to be 20 years of age with a high school diploma or GED.

After the initial application, each department follows a process that includes cognitive testing, physical abilities evaluation, background assessments, drug assessments, polygraph or other lie detection methods and psychological evaluation. It should be noted these three departments represent a large police department within each state and their requirements may be very different from a smaller police department consisting of only a few officers. Smaller police departments, with limited budgets, may find it financially difficult to require psychological testing and may find it unnecessary to require a stringent physical abilities evaluation.

Cognitive testing can evaluate the applicant's ability to read, understand and process information, ability to memorize and organize information in addition to basic math skills. Some of these tests may be timed to evaluate a recruit's performance under pressure. A police officer is required to process, organize, memorize and evaluate information quickly. It is important to determine someone's ability to accomplish these tasks early in the process. Some departments utilize scenarios to paint a visual picture and require applicants to process that information before being asked about the details of the scenario. For example, an applicant may be shown five photographs of people and later asked to describe one of the people depicted in one of the photographs without looking back at the photographs. The following is an example of how this line of questioning can be used in the daily activities of police officers. An officer witnesses a white male walk into a bank wearing a long black coat and red gym shoes; however, it isn't cold outside. A few minutes later after the officer leaves the area of the bank, he is notified of a robbery at the same bank. The description is given of a white male wearing a long black coat. The officer drives around the area but doesn't locate the white male wearing a long black coat. He does observe the same white male he observed previously entering the bank wearing a long black coat and red gym shoes; however, the man was now wearing khaki shorts, blue and red stripe shirt and red gym shoes. The male was detained and found to be carrying a bank bag, containing money, in his backpack. The officer was able to process the information he received when he observed the male walk into the bank and utilized that information to locate a suspect.

    Background evaluations are designed to determine if there are any activities in an applicant's past that would disqualify them for employment. Some departments rely heavily on credit reports. Credit reports can not only give an indication of whether you pay your bills it also provides insight into someone's ability to accept responsibility. A credit report that has multiple open lines of revolving credit (credit cards) with large balances and late payments in addition to liens and judgments can indicate a person's inability to maintain financial responsibility. During my application process, I asked why a credit report was important and I was told someone with bad credit would be more susceptible to bribery. Whether it indicates susceptibility to bribery or financial responsibility, a good credit report is a requirement for some agencies. A driving record provides information about citations received for driving infractions as well as motor vehicle accidents the applicant may have been involved in. An applicant who has multiple citations for speeding or other moving violations may indicate an applicant's disregard for traffic laws. An applicant who has shown their inability to adhere to the laws they will be expected to enforce may be eliminated from the hiring process.

As indicated, larger police departments ensure their application process includes diverse methods to screen and eliminate those applicants who are unfit for the position. These multiple layers of evaluations can ensure a more thorough screening process to ensure applicants are not able to gain employment by deceiving one portion of the process. There may be some instances in which an applicant can fool an interview panel but may not be able to deceive a polygraph examiner or a psychologist. For example, an applicant with negative biases towards a group of people may be able to deceive a polygraph or an interview panel; however, an effective psychological exam may reveal those biases and cause the applicant to be eliminated from the process.

Negative drug screenings and untruthfulness have continued to make a law enforcement career for some candidates elusive. As more and more states move towards legalizing marijuana, law enforcement has not wavered in the requirement of their applicants to be drug-free. I had a conversation with a police chief of a small Georgia police department about recruiting. His stance was that they were getting good applicants, but they lost them because of marijuana. Candidates who completed the employment application and background packet were asked if they ever used marijuana. Most people, when they get to this question, may feel they will be denied employment if they respond truthfully by stating they have used marijuana, so they lie and say they have not. The application is processed, and the applicant is scheduled for a polygraph examination. Questions involving drug use will ALWAYS be asked, and it is imperative that an applicant is honest in their responses. In most instances, applicants are very honest and forthcoming during these examinations, and that is the problem. When an applicant indicates they have not used drugs, to include marijuana, on an application and then tells a polygraph examiner they have used drugs the applicant is eliminated from the process for being dishonest.

I will never forget the polygraph examination I took when I applied for my first law enforcement position. As a high school student, I was always too afraid to try marijuana. During those years there were news stories about marijuana being mixed with mind altering chemicals. Although many of my classmates indulged in marijuana, I declined to be around anyone smoking marijuana, and that fear has continued to this day. I remember completing my application and speaking with the recruitment sergeant who asked, " Are you sure you have never smoked marijuana?" I responded proudly " Nope; I have never tried it." She went on to say if I had and it was a long time ago it is ok to say I had tried it before. I continued " No ma'am, I have never tried it."

The look she gave me was as if she just knew I was lying. When I got to the polygraph, the examiner asked if I had ever used drugs and I responded, "No." He asked a few other questions and came back to the drug question, and I answered, "No" again. After the polygraph was completed, he told me that he observed signs of deception about the drug question. He asked again if I had ever used drugs and I told him I had not. The examiner laid it on pretty thick about deceiving the exam. He almost made me believe I had actually smoked marijuana. After that experience, I can see why innocent people confess to crimes they never committed. Later in my career, I met a polygraph examiner who was willing to share his secrets of success. I told him about the examiner telling me he observed deception when I was telling the truth. I was then informed, an examiner attempts to get an applicant or examinee to admit to deceiving the exam by indicating they observed deception even if they did not. In other words, it was the last ploy at getting me to admit to something I had not done. There was no doubt in his mind that me being about twentyish and had never smoked marijuana was impossible.

A thorough application process that includes multiple methods of screening can have a positive impact on the type of person who might be employed by a police department.

Basic Training

After someone successfully completes the application process and they are hired by a police department they are sent to a basic training school to learn the skills necessary to perform the duties of a police officer. Large police departments like New York City Police (NYPD), Los Angeles Police Department (LAPD) and Atlanta Police Department (APD) have their own police academies where they have the discretion in formatting their basic training academies to the specific training needs of their department. Although these academies have discretion in the format of their classes, guidelines in the content taught could be mandated by each state. Smaller police departments may send their trainees to a state or regional academy, rather than assume the cost of basic training. Unlike a departmental basic training academy, a state or regional academy is unable to relate the training provided to specific needs of any particular department or community.

The basic training school is where the police officer develops the basic skills and knowledge necessary to establish a foundation of policing principles. Basic training schools begin by impressing upon the trainee a strict chain of command. Trainees must understand from day one who is in charge. This is the beginning of their indoctrination into the para-military model of policing. The team philosophy is instilled in each trainee as they are taught to depend on each other, that law enforcement is a family and that the thin blue line is representative of that family. Firearms training, driving, state law and use of force are four categories that are consistent in every basic training school regardless of location. Lately, there has been an emphasis on preparing officers for interactions with mentally disabled persons through crisis intervention training (CIT). The manner these subject areas are taught and the time spent on each topic varies across the country. Generally, these academy classes heavily depend on a lecture, as some are unequipped to provide detailed life-like scenarios for each aspect of training. It is impossible for officers or trainees to train for every possible incident. However, it would be beneficial for officers to engage in practical exercises that reenact a variety of situations. Discussing multiple possible reactions and outcomes related to those reactions is also an important component to this type of training. Officers should be encouraged to think freely and make mistakes in the academy so when provided similar real world incidents they make effective decisions.

Recent, highly televised incidents involving uses of force and uses of deadly force by police has caused the public to insist on additional training for officers in areas such as interacting with mentally disabled citizens and incident de-escalation. Although an officer should be able to de-escalate a situation using effective communication, that concept totally contradicts the command and control philosophy that is taught in the academy. As a police trainee, I was taught when we arrive at a scene, we must take control of that scene and command compliance. Failure to comply with an officer's commands sometimes results in the officer using force to gain compliance. If the participants of the disturbance get loud, the police may get louder because they should be in control. If participants display actions of aggression police may respond with aggression. When teaching this command and control philosophy characteristics of various cultures should be taught as well.

In the academy when we talked about cultural differences we always spent a lot of time on the Asian culture and how they believe looking someone in the eye is disrespectful, but we never talked about how people of certain cultures, races, ethnicities, genders, sexual orientations and socioeconomic backgrounds responded to the police. When I was a patrol officer, I found different people responded to situations differently, which required me to respond differently. In one incident I responded to a disturbance in a home occupied by an African American family. The involved parties spoke loud, cursed and used hand gestures as they were telling me what occurred. I knew their intent was not to disrespect me or my authority, but they were angry, and in telling their story their words and gestures reflected that anger. Their actions were simply a display of emotion. Some officers might see those actions as defying their ability to gain control of the situation. I found as the residents continued to speak their voices began to get softer, the cursing subsided, and the hand gestures stopped. There was no need for me to shout and threaten to arrest them or tell them a hundred times to calm down. Some officers might have been unable to allow the residents to naturally calm down and rather than listen through the cursing they might decide to arrest the residents for disorderly conduct. The officer is taught they cannot help until they gain control and the parties involved are compliant. A mature officer, someone who has experience and empathy, may handle the incident differently by telling the family member in a calm voice "Hey I understand you are upset. I want to help you, but first I have to understand what happened." At this time the officer has to listen through the shouting and hand gestures because continuing to yell at the person telling them to calm down is counterproductive and an arrest would be an injustice. An officer should not have to be on the job for 4 to 5 years before they realize the best way to build rapport with someone is to do so with respect, understanding, and empathy. At the same time, citizens have to understand officers are taught to command control of an incident and gain compliance regardless of what type of incident it is. I worked with an officer, and his way of showing he was in charge was arriving at the incident location, pulling his pants up, pushing his shoulders back, adjusting his police vest around his neck and telling the person who called "Ok, you called me. Now I'm in charge so listen to me." He was taking command and letting people know he was in control but he was rude, and the way he spoke was demeaning. The officer failed to be respectful and thus a disrespectful response was often returned. Both police officers and citizens have to understand how a command and control philosophy lacking effective communication and non-compliance, can negatively impact police/citizen encounters.

Use of force and use of deadly force incidents have continued to divide the country on either the police side or the community side. I have attended forums on police use of force that were totally ineffective as the topic centered around the problem and rarely discussed viable solutions. Before a solution can be obtained there has to be an understanding of the issue by both sides. Notice I did not say agreement. If the police fail to truly understand why communities have a problem they cannot assist in solving the problem. If community members fail to truly understand the job of a police officer and how that job is performed they cannot assist in solving the problem. It is not necessary to agree on these issues, but there has to be a mutual understanding. In some communities, police agencies have failed to effectively convey their role and how they are willing to address the issue with officer's use of force. This can only be accomplished through training and education on both sides of the issue.

An article by Paul Waldman included an interview with Maria Haberfeld of the John Jay College of Criminal Justice, in which Haberfeld indicated there are not nearly enough resources provided for officer use of force training. She contends that the training law enforcement agencies provide do not address the emotional, psychological and social impacts of police use of force incidents. Incidents that involve the use of force, especially use of deadly force, cannot and should not be grouped together for comparison; however, the cause for each incident can be evaluated individually and training can be developed to understand and address any misconceptions officers may have when encountering similar incidents. Each incident involves multiple variables that make each incident unique. One obvious difference in an incident is the officer involved, which provides for a number of possible differences, such as age, maturity, education level, type and amount of training received, number of years on the job, personality and other factors. These variables do not include the target of the use of force or the environment. Based on just the officer variables alone there is no way these incidents can be grouped for comparison. You can, however, evaluate each incident independently for justification.

Training is a very necessary and important part of a career in law enforcement. The training obtained in a basic training academy cannot support an officer for their entire career. There has to be ongoing, relevant training throughout a police career. As laws, procedures and philosophies change officers should maintain a mastery of the complexities of these issues. The police officer is a position in which a person is expected to counsel people through issues but is not required to have the advanced education that someone like a social worker or a teacher is required to have. Police departments make an honorable attempt at developing officers into well-rounded people who can adapt to various situations and provide accurate information to assist people in solving their issues. They ensure their officer trainees have support as they maneuver through the basic academy. They provide the trainee with a field training officer upon completion of the academy to enhance the skills learned in the basic academy and allow them the opportunity to utilize those skills in real world experiences. The department provides professional development training which also provides the officer additional training in areas the department deems important. Most departments accomplish this training utilizing senior officers who have had specialized POLICE training in a variety of areas. Professional development at my last agency was conducted by the training department over two days with a variety of topics. The training was just enough to say it had been done, but none provided the in-depth training that was needed due to a lack of time available to allow officers to be away from the field. There was an outside instructor that conducted an introductory class on interacting with mentally disabled persons. It was good to be introduced to the topic by a professional as the training was excellent. The instructor was engaging and she was able to relate the topic to police duties, but there was not enough time spent on the topic. I'm sure this happens in a large number of departments across the country.

There are barriers to departments providing adequate, effective, ongoing and relevant training. Obtaining experienced professionals to conduct police related training can be difficult. Although there may be plenty of psychologists who can provide training to officers related to interacting with mentally disabled persons, the issue comes about when the training is not relevant to the police job. Officers are skeptical about training from people who have no idea what it is they do and the issues they are faced with in the field. Thus, they are reluctant to listen and may dismiss the training as necessary but irrelevant. It takes a mature officer, who can step outside the type A personality and ask questions, so they have a clear understanding of the topics discussed. They can take the information and relate it to the police job. They can also create effective lesson plans and can teach the information to officers, making it relevant and easy for them to understand. Some departments accomplish this by having management and supervisors attend these type of trainings along with their training department. The problem with this approach is management and supervisors are so far removed from field work that they may not be able to relate what they have learned to the issues the patrol officer may see daily. Also, training staff may have also been removed from the field thus making their ability to relate the training difficult. It would be a good idea to include officers who have the respect of their peers in such training opportunities and charge them with assisting in the development of department training in that area.

Cost is another huge barrier to officer training. The cost of attending specialized training has grown as costs for travel grows. Generally, if a subject matter expert is requested to provide training at a department, that department may be required to foot the bill for travel, hotel, meals in addition to the payment for the actual training. The more experienced the person conducting the training, the more the training will cost. I have seen advertisements for training that costs up to $1500 per person for a two-day class.

Smaller departments just do not have the training budgets to send their officers to these types of specialized training. Some states have the ability to send state trainers to this type of training and then provide the training for multiple officers around the state without a cost to the officer or department, but these state trainers are career teachers and have in some cases been removed from field work for years as well.

Another barrier to obtaining police training is having adequate personnel coverage while allowing officers to attend training. A police chief cannot justify not having enough officers on patrol because they had to attend training. The job of providing a safe environment has to be the top priority of the department. The million dollar question is how can a community be safe when the officers charged with providing that safety are not adequately trained? The answer, in short, is the officers are adequately trained, according to state mandates. As the potential employee pool for police departments decrease the opportunities for advanced training also decreases. This has been and continues to be a thorn in the side of police administrators. As communities across the country urge agencies to implement more training for officers, it is important to understand the process may be a slow one as there are many barriers that can make obtaining training a difficult task.

Personal Academy Experience

My training academy experience was amazing. I met a lot of great people who shared a unique desire to dedicate their lives to protecting and serving strangers. Just as I began the academy tragedy struck my family. My father died after a long bout with kidney complications. My academy class, who had only known me for a short period, collected money to send me home for the funeral. I left my biological family after burying my father and returned to my law enforcement family which was comprised of sheriff deputy recruits and police officer recruits. These men and women became my family away from home. We developed a bond which, at that time, was unbroken. We believed in the thin blue line, that all law enforcement officers were family, and we must keep each other safe. Although this was a wonderful and exciting time for me in the academy, I began to feel my old friends slip away. My thought processes changed and trust for people, in general, began to decrease. The police academy made me much more hypersensitive to what was going on around me. I was more aware of my surroundings and the potential danger that loomed. When dining out, I began to request and locate seating where I could have a view of the doors. I began to play scenarios in my head to anticipate how I would respond to various situations, using the training that I received daily. I noticed myself giving safety advice to my friends and family on a regular basis. I had embarked on a new career, and I was learning some exciting stuff, or so I thought. I was taken aback when my friends and family were not as excited to hear about the things I was learning in the academy. How do you share your experiences with the people you care about if they don't really feel the excitement you feel? This was the beginning of the isolation that some officers feel throughout their career. I found myself being in the company of police officers and other public safety employees, like firefighters and paramedics, but mostly police officers. I found that I had limited perspectives about worldly issues. I had tunnel vision and could only see things through a law enforcement lens. My conversations were limited to work related issues, replaying tragic incidents over and over in conversations. I could no longer see the big picture. It wasn't until I had been on the job for about 4 or 5 years that I realized my law enforcement only relationships were unhealthy. It was that point that I began to reach past my comfort zones and interact with a more diverse crowd. My new friends were more well-rounded and represented a multitude of career fields, political views, and religious backgrounds. As I changed, the manner in which I approached my job changed. I began to have more empathy for the people I was charged with protecting and serving.

    We began the first day of the academy with an introduction to military structure by learning to line up into ranks. Those who did not put a glossy shine on their shoes and a crease in the pants and shirt were ridiculed by instructors. We were told the class leadership would be chosen by instructors. There was a group of about 5 or six trainees that came from one department, and it appeared they had already decided one of their folks would be the president of our class. One of the trainees from that department was always shouting at everyone and getting people in line; he was apparently a military guy. He was chosen as president, and I was chosen as vice president. There was not one moment that he did not refer to me as "his" vice president.

We spent time in the classroom learning law and criminal procedures. We discussed use of force and use of deadly force, but there were not many practical exercises that would provide the psychological, physiological and emotional impacts that would result from the use of force. Today there are simulation machines, interactive video and virtual reality programs that provide the officer with an opportunity to train in judgmental shooting and accuracy. The officer is presented with a video that depicts a real world incident. The officer responds armed with a simulation weapon that is paired with the machine. Using the machine and weapon, the officer is presented with incidents that either requires them to use deadly force or not use deadly force. Usually, this type of training is conducted by a firearms instructor who controls the direction the scenario will take. An example of this type of training might be an incident in which an officer responds to a suspicious person call that depicts a male with clown face paint hanging out in front of a bank. The male tells the officer they are waiting on someone inside the bank. The officer tells the man to keep his hands to his side as he is speaking with the man. The man reaches into his coat, ignoring the officer's command to keep his hands at his sides, and pulls out a gun that appears to be real. The officer draws his weapon and fires, killing the man. The officer later found the gun the clown possessed was a water pistol. The officer found himself with a split second decision in which he perceived a threat and fired the weapon to stop the threat. There are some police departments that are holding training in which the public is allowed to participate in the simulation training in an attempt to help people understand how quickly officers have to make these decisions. I highly recommend taking an opportunity to participate in this type of training if it is offered in your community.

My class spent a lot of time at the gun range working on stationary targets that only turned away and back towards us. We learned about the weapons we were going to carry, the parts, how to break them down, how to clean them, how to carry them and most importantly, how to retain them in a struggle. Firearms instructors have attempted to make firearms training more realistic by implementing courses of fire in which officers are required to move and to utilize items that will provide them adequate cover in a gun fight.

We learned how to utilize our hands to defend ourselves. It was not like a martial arts class, but we did learn a few techniques to utilize when faced with passive resistance. During that class we also learned how to effectively get someone who was resisting arrest into handcuffs but as I remember the training was more of physical means to gain compliance and not as much communicating the person into the handcuffs.

We were taught how to conduct a traffic stop, how to respond to domestic disturbances and the dangers that could arise from those incidents. The most fun activity we did was operating an emergency vehicle. We drove through a timed cone course where we were tested on parking, driving forward and backward avoiding obstacles, turning at high speeds, braking at high speeds, stopping abruptly and handling a vehicle during a skid. It all caused me to be a better, more aware, defensive driver but it also seemed to make me drive a lot faster, at the same time being safe (yes it's possible).

There were written tests every week that evaluated our comprehension of the subject matter for that week. We were required to make an acceptable score on all of the written exams in addition to satisfactorily completing the range and driving courses. Although the exams were weekly, the firearms test was week three or four and the driving test was near the end, in week nine or ten of the eleven week academy. Failure to perform satisfactorily in those areas would disqualify a trainee from continuing.

After successful graduation from the training academy, I went back to my department where I was assigned a field training officer. I was eager, energetic and ready to get going applying what I had learned but the officer I was assigned to was reluctant to train me. We didn't do much patrolling. We responded to the calls we were dispatched to which were not very many as we were on the morning watch, a shift that began at midnight and ended at 8 am. For the most part every night we sat at one of those all night breakfast restaurants. After a few weeks of that, I went to the department training coordinator and complained about the lack of training I was being provided. A couple of weeks after that I was reassigned to that officer's on-duty-buddy. This guy had a different approach to training. We got out of the car and walked. He showed me paths that suspects used to flee and evade police. We climbed through windows of abandoned homes and buildings. We made traffic stops. We did a lot of great training. To this date I believe initially the methods of training he used were to make me complain or quit but he quickly saw that I was not some apprehensive lazy female who just wanted to ride around and do nothing. I appreciated the time he took explaining why we did what we did, providing constructive criticism and being a positive influence on my police career. I had and have respect for that guy for being such a well-rounded officer. He was knowledgeable in multiple aspects of policing, which is necessary for a field training officer. After the change in training officers my field training experience was the best and one of the most memorable experiences in my law enforcement career. The training I had been provided molded my career and contributed to the desire I have had in being a well-rounded and knowledgeable police officer.

6
SEARCH AND SEIZURE

Rule 6: *Many of the issues that arise with citizen/police interactions come during either a search or a seizure. There are certain requirements that must be present for a search or seizure. Knowing those requirements can help foster positive interactions.*

Fourth Amendment to the United States Constitution

"The right of the people to be secure in their persons, houses, papers, and effects, against unreasonable searches and seizures, shall not be violated, and no warrants shall issue, but upon probable cause, supported by oath or affirmation, and particularly describing the place to be searched, and the persons or things to be seized." -United States Constitution

There is a lot of legal jargon within the Constitution making it a little difficult to understand the rights afforded to people within the United States. As a police officer, in the course of my duties, I often heard citizens say "I know my rights. I have the right to do this, and I have the right to do that." But, in most cases, they were wrong in what they believed they knew about their Constitutional Rights.

Although there are several Constitutional Rights that are involved in the course of an officer's duties this chapter discusses one very important one, the right of the people to be secure in their persons, houses, papers, and effects against unreasonable search and seizure. Further, it includes that our belongings will not be searched without a warrant that includes support by oath or affirmation. There are requirements that a law enforcement officer MUST meet before obtaining an arrest or search warrant. One of those requirements and the most important is probable cause (PC). There must be a set of facts and circumstances that would lead a reasonable person to believe that a crime has occurred. Probable cause is very different from articulable reasonable suspicion (ARS). An officer's probable cause should be clear enough that an average citizen could read it and understand a crime has been committed; whereas ARS can only be articulated by a law enforcement officer based on their knowledge, training, and experience. ARS can be used as a building block to an arrest; however, it cannot stand on its own as a justification for an arrest. There must be probable cause present to arrest someone.

    When I think about the word secure I see myself being without intrusion, whether it is intrusion into my personal space, my vehicle, my home, my phone, computer, files, etc. I, as well as my belongings, should be safe from people which include police officers from entering my home uninvited or examining my belongings without my permission. The Fourth Amendment guarantees this. But, how can an average person ensure their rights are recognized by law enforcement personnel? Knowledge, not only about your rights but how those rights are interpreted and applied.

Police officers are charged with learning various rights guaranteed by the U.S. Constitution and how they should conduct themselves to ensure the rights of the citizens they encounter are acknowledged and preserved. For most officers, the academy experience is a re-introduction to the United States Constitution, a refresher from a high school civics class or a college political science class. During the academy, recruits are expected to learn how to apply the rights afforded in the Constitution justly in the course of their duties. Recruits are expected to show they have mastered the skills introduced to them while in the training academy through a variety of testing and evaluation methods.

The United States Constitution reads... *To be secure in their persons, houses, papers, and effects, against unreasonable searches...* There are many facets that are involved with searching a person, their belongings, and their home. As these intrusions are made daily throughout the country, court cases are adjudicated and present us with case law that guides law enforcement in their application of this very important right. While the Constitution indicates we will be secure from unreasonable search it is the case law that defines what is reasonable and what is unreasonable through exceptions. For example, it is reasonable to search a carryon bag before it is taken onto a plane. This is reasonable because an airplane search is an exception to the unreasonable search portion of the Constitution. The Supreme Court has heard many cases related to searches of people and their property and have determined there are certain exceptions to these rules that define when a search can and cannot occur.

There are several exceptions related to reasonable searches. Some of the most used ones are:

1. **Airport Searches:** Searches of your person and baggage within the airport are legal. Each time you enter a security checkpoint at an airport you are subject to a search and must comply, or you will not be allowed to proceed.

2. **Vehicle Searches:** Your vehicle can be searched provided there is probable cause to search. Any closed, locked, or otherwise secure bags, boxes, etc. cannot be searched without a warrant. Vehicle searches are often proposed during traffic stops. Probable cause for a vehicle search could be something as minor as the smell of marijuana. If the officer smells it, they can search your vehicle. A good rule to follow is, do not smoke marijuana in your vehicle. Although some jurisdictions have moved to decriminalize possession of marijuana, some jurisdictions have not and continue to utilize drug interdiction stops to write citations and make arrests for possession of marijuana.

3. **Consent Searches:** If you give your consent to search your person or property the search is legal. Remember anytime you give consent you can take that consent away at any time whether you give consent to search your vehicle, your home, your electronic devices or other belongings. If, at some point, prior to you telling the police to stop searching

they locate something that is illegal (contraband) they will then have probable cause to arrest. In some instances, officers who locate a small piece of contraband that equates to probable cause may discontinue their search to obtain a search warrant. It is always better for an officer to be more cautious by obtaining a search warrant.

4. **Plain View:** If the officer sees evidence of a crime in plain view they now have probable cause for an arrest. Plain view means the officer sees the evidence without moving or manipulating anything to obtain the view of the evidence.

5. **Abandoned Property:** Abandoned property can be searched. For example, you may place bloody clothes you were wearing in a trashcan, and on Wednesday you put the trashcan out on the curb. Officers can search the trash because as it sits on the curb awaiting pickup. There is no expectation of privacy. It has been abandoned.

6. **Search After an Arrest (Search incident to arrest):** If you are arrested, you and your property can be searched. If there is a locked container, smart phone, computer, etc. the officer must obtain a search warrant to search the property.

7. **Administrative Searches:** The most common administrative search is an inventory of a vehicle. An example of this type of search would be if a person is arrested and the officer impounds the vehicle—their department policy may direct them to conduct an inventory of the vehicle. They would simply list everything of value

that was inside the vehicle and any visible damage to the vehicle. In some agencies, the officer allows the suspect to locate a suitable person to turn the vehicle over to rather than impounding the vehicle.

Stop and Frisk policies of the New York Police Department (NYPD) were known to have been extremely controversial and against a person's rights as it pertains to unreasonable search and seizure. The policy allowed NYPD officers to arbitrarily stop citizens, interview them and search them on the street with mere articulable reasonable suspicion; hence the name stop and frisk. This type of stop was referred to as a Terry Stop; based on *US Supreme Court case Terry v Ohio*. A Terry Stop is based on reasonable articulable suspicion which is a set of facts and circumstances that would lead a reasonable law enforcement officer, who, relying on their knowledge, training, and experience to believe a crime had been committed or was about to be committed. Although Terry Stops are a common tool utilized by law enforcement to combat criminal activity, it must combine the facts that would lead a reasonable officer to believe a crime has been or is about to be committed in addition to the reasonable belief that the person suspected of the criminal activity is armed. The stop and frisk policy gained immense scrutiny among Black and Latino communities as the practice equated to racial profiling.

Litigation against the racial profiling practices of New York Police Department began in 1999 with a class action lawsuit filed by The Center for Constitutional Rights in United States District

Court for the Southern District of New York (CCR). The case was in response to the practice and policies of the NYPD in their stopping and frisking of minority citizens. The case surrounded specific activities of a specialized unit within the NYPD Street Crimes Unit (SCU). Many of the stops made by this unit were baseless and did not meet the requirements of previous case law in *Terry v Ohio*. According to CCR, in 1997 and 1998, 35,000 of the 45,000 stop and frisks reported by the NYPD Street Crimes Unit did not result in an arrest. The case was won by the plaintiffs and resulted in the disbanding of the Street Crimes Unit (ccrjustice.org).

Because the stop and frisk practice did not cease The Center for Constitutional Rights filed an additional class action lawsuit; Floyd, et al. v. City of New York, et al. The case was in response to the continued pattern of racial profiling during stop and frisk encounters with NYPD officers. The case was finally settled, and a collaborative community effort began to establish viable solutions (ccrjustice.org).

New York City Police Department was not alone in their interpretations of search and seizure. There were police departments in other metropolitan areas that had crime suppression units that were notorious for 3 or 4 officers exiting their patrol vehicles and ordering people to stand against walls, lie on the ground, or just stand there with their hands in the air. Those police units were responsible for maintaining order in the rough streets of urban metropolitan areas. In some instances, these officers searched suspected drug dealers for drugs and weapons without probable cause or warrants. This behavior was prevalent before the use of cellphone cameras and the creation of countless social media sites. During those times officers were given *carte blanche* to stop whomever and do whatever they desired. Officers would routinely stop people who were standing on corners, in front of store fronts or in front of apartment complexes, places that were identified as high drug, high crime areas. The officers would search the suspect's pockets for drugs. If nothing was found the citizen would be free to leave. Drug dealers learned quickly to refrain from storing narcotics in their pockets because they would be easily located during a search by police. Those drug dealers began to hide narcotics inside their underwear even underneath their testicles. This was a great hiding place because any search of someone's underwear would be very intrusive and such a search would not be legal under *Terry v. Ohio*.

While drug dealers learned from their mistakes and adapted to police practices, police officers also adapted by changing the manner in which they searched for narcotics. These searches consisted of requiring suspects to open their pants, exposing their genitals to determine if they were in possession of narcotics. During some of these searches, suspects were asked to manipulate their genitals so the officer could determine if narcotics were present. Females were not excluded from the illegal, intrusive searches; however, female officers were utilized to search female suspects who were thought to possess narcotics inside their underwear. None of these practices are legal under Terry; however, citizen consent may have been used to avoid the appearance of an illegal search.

It is important that officers who are charged with searching suspects who enter a jail be allowed to conduct a thorough search of their property and person to ensure contraband is not brought into a secure jail environment. A search conducted after an arrest, also referred to as search incident to arrest, is legal and does not require consent. However, a search of someone's body cavity is a more intrusive search. It should be noted a search of someone's genitals in jail is totally different from an arbitrary search on the side of the road in which there is no probable cause. If an officer has probable cause to arrest a suspect they should be placed in handcuffs before the search. The officer should limit the time on the side of the road searching suspects but should ensure they conduct a thorough search to locate any weapons that could be used against them. The side of the road search is an embarrassment to the suspect and a safety hazard to the officer. The more time an officer takes to interact with a suspect who will ultimately be arrested while they are on the side of the road equates to more opportunity for a suspect to take flight or begin a physical assault on the officer. Officers have been assaulted while attempting to place suspects in handcuffs. There have also been incidents in which suspects have fled while in handcuffs as they are being searched by officers.

A body cavity search is very intrusive and requires a search warrant in which a judge decides whether there is sufficient probable cause to grant such a search. In some cases, suspects who were subjected to unreasonable body cavity searches sued the responsible departments. These unreasonable search practices are not taught through official training by law enforcement agencies. However, some veteran officers pass on their personal knowledge and behaviors to new (fresh out of the academy) officers. New officers are told by their veteran training officers to forget everything they have learned in the academy because the streets are different than the academy. The academy experience is different. It provides the officer with the tactical, cognitive and educational foundation that guides them in the performance of their duties while the field training experience provides an opportunity to apply what was learned under the close supervision of the field training officer. It is during this phase in a young officer's career that they are shaped and molded. They learn how to interact with people within the communities they serve but how they will perform independently is formed from their own moral fortitude.

Why do officers knowingly violate people's rights? In some cases, the officer may not be experienced enough or have retained the knowledge to know that their actions are in violation of some Constitutional Right. In other cases, the officer may believe their actions will not be detected and (or) punished. Yet, in other cases, the officer may have seen some other officer, usually, a senior officer, display the same actions and believe that the unlawful, unethical actions are acceptable in that environment. There are also those officers who are just not concerned with some citizen's Constitutional Rights.

A seizure can be of a person or property. Seizing a person can be related to an arrest or a shooting. If a person is arrested, they are considered to be seized. If a person is shot, they are considered to be seized. The seizure of a person is also dictated by the Fourth Amendment which describes a person's right against the unreasonable search and seizure of their property and (or) their person. Further, a person cannot be seized without probable cause or a warrant issued based on probable cause. A seizure of a person (arrest) is not the same as an investigatory stop. After being arrested, the suspect is not free to leave without posting a bond or paying a fine. If an officer shoots a person, they are considered to be seizing the person and thus must have probable cause when doing so. The force used to effect (make) an arrest must be justified by the crime committed. For example, an officer cannot justify shooting a suspected shoplifter unless it is known the shoplifter is armed and they pose a threat to the officer or someone else. This is why it is imperative that citizens listen and follow an officer's verbal directions. When citizens deviate from the directions the officer provides it is sometimes perceived by the officer as a threat, causing the officer to use force to stop the threat. These acts may include using hands on tactics (fighting); less-lethal weapons such as pepper spray and batons or electroshock weapons. Finally, depending on the perceived threat an officer can utilize a firearm to stop a threat. The important thing to know about seizing a person is there must be probable cause or a **perceived** threat.

During the Basic Academy, classroom lectures that outlined when an officer has the authority to use deadly force were anchored by the United States Constitution and emphasizing previous Supreme Court cases, referred to as case law. A very important case, *Tennessee v. Garner,* was used to teach a concept that is at the forefront of several controversial killings of unarmed people by law enforcement. *Tennessee v. Garner* is known as the fleeing felon case. The incident that led to the Supreme Court case took place in Memphis, Tennessee where state law allowed officers to use deadly force to prevent a suspect from fleeing or forcibly resisting arrest but only after an officer informed the suspect of the intention to make an arrest. The case centered around Edward Garner who was inside someone's home committing a theft which is considered burglary and a felony. Upon the arrival of Officer Elton Hymon, Garner fled the home and approached a chain-link fence. Hymon, using his flashlight, recognized Garner was not armed. Hymon identified himself as a police officer and gave Garner verbal commands to stop. After Garner began to climb the fence Officer Hymon fired his gun striking Garner in the back of his head. Garner later died in the hospital. Garner's father sought civil action in Federal Court; however, the court ruled based on Tennessee law that Hymon acted lawfully in preventing the escape of Garner by shooting him. The court concluded that Garner's attempt to flee caused his death. The Court of Appeals reversed the decision of the District Court and found shooting Garner was considered a seizure, under the Fourth Amendment, and thus the seizure must be reasonable. It further decided that it was not reasonable to seize Garner (use deadly force) as he did not pose a threat to Officer Hymon or the community at large (a third party). The state of Tennessee appealed to The Supreme Court which ruled, the use of deadly force against an unarmed suspect, who posed no threat to the officer or community was unreasonable. A very important caveat to the Supreme Court ruling was if there was probable cause that the suspect caused or threatened serious physical harm to the officer or a third party deadly force would be justified. Consequently, the Supreme Court case decision has provided somewhat of a guide to officers in their utilization of deadly force. This is a very important concept for average citizens to understand. It appears that each ruling by the Supreme Court, about law enforcement, echoes a theme of reasonableness.

This court case continues to be a cornerstone of law enforcement training in the use of deadly force.

Use of deadly force is taught in basic academies; however, just as with the other topics the manner of instruction and time spent on topic varies. The lecture portion that involves understanding Constitutional Rights, case law and criminal procedures is coupled by some departments with judgmental shooting training. In many incidents, officers are forced to make life and death decisions in split seconds. They must process a number of things. Their decisions are based upon their perception of the situation at that time coupled with their knowledge, training, experience and their desire to return home to their family. Judgmental shooting allows the officer to practice their split second life and death decision making skills while utilizing manually controlled video simulation which provides the officer with real world scenarios. The simulation further allows officers to see their mistakes without placing the officer or the public in harm's way.

It should be understood by citizens that policing is a very dangerous job. Officers value their lives as they value the oath they made to protect and serve but the ultimate goal of an officer is to return home to their families just as they arrived to begin their tour of duty.

7
Vehicular Encounters

Rule 7: *Vehicular encounters are more prevalent as citizens may be more likely to encounter a law enforcement officer on a traffic stop than during any other time. Knowing what is required of a driver and their passengers can be beneficial to promoting a positive interaction.*

Police officers encounter citizens in a number of ways, a variety of environments and for various reasons. One occasion in which officers encounter citizens is during a traffic stop. This is generally when an officer has observed some traffic related infraction and has to make contact with the driver. Instances that may cause an officer to pull a vehicle over include moving violations and (or) equipment violations.

When an officer is killed or seriously injured while conducting a traffic stop, the media oftentimes refers to it as a "routine traffic stop". Although on the surface it may seem as if all traffic stops are the same this could not be further from the truth. Every traffic stop is different unless the same officer is stopping the same person, at the same time of day, in the same location, under the same conditions, etc. Even with all the same conditions the traffic stop would be different because both the officer and the driver would have had different experiences on one day compared to another day.

Traffic stops differ because of human factors, environmental factors and other circumstances that are constantly changing. If the officer making the traffic stop had a bad experience prior to that stop, the stop could be negatively influenced. Likewise, if the driver had a bad experience prior to the stop, this could also negatively influence the stop. In contrast, if either party had a pleasant experience prior to the stop, this could positively influence the stop. If the officer had to pull you over in the rain, causing them to get drenched, that could probably negatively influence the stop. In essence, our attitudes can sometimes determine how well or how bad a traffic stop goes. It is important to remember a person can only be in control of themselves. If faced with a police/citizen encounter do your best to ensure it is a positive one. In some cases one party may have to over compensate their positivity to counter the negativity of the other person. The best thing to do, if you are faced with an officer with a nasty attitude, is to be positive, remain pleasant and calm. The worst thing a person can do is match a bad attitude with a bad attitude. The second worst thing either party could do during a traffic stop is to crack open their bag of sarcasm.

    The police officer, unless they are in training, has discretion which means they often have a choice in the actions they take. If they are in training they are usually told by a senior officer what actions they are to take. In most instances the officer has a choice whether to write a citation or not for traffic offenses. However, other violations may require bail be posted. The traffic stop is an instance in which an officer may issue a citation in lieu of posting a bond; which means, the driver's signature is all the officer will need for the driver to continue on their way.

A driver should know what to expect when they are stopped by a police officer. I would love to include professionalism here; however, that is not always the case. If a driver is faced with an unprofessional officer remember you can always make a formal complaint. Remain calm and pleasant. It is not inconceivable for an officer to make the traffic stop last longer and be more unpleasant than it should be.

Once an officer observes a violation, they may check the tag information on a mobile computer prior to pulling a vehicle over. If a driver observes a marked police vehicle following them for a few minutes, this could be the reason. If you want to determine if the officer is following you signal and change lanes. If the officer follows you to the next lane, you should probably prepare to be pulled over.

> **Note:** Although changing lanes is not against the law if done properly, some officers consider sudden lane changes suspicious behavior. If you decide to change lanes signal first and then slowly change lanes.

Checking a tag prior to pulling a vehicle over is done for two very important reasons. The first is to determine if the vehicle is stolen and the second is to determine if the registered vehicle owner may have an outstanding warrant. This is accomplished by running the tag number through the NCIC system, which simultaneously runs the tag through the state Crime Information Center. The returned information from the tag check includes the registered owner name, address, date of birth, vehicle make, model, VIN number, registration expiration, whether the vehicle is insured and by whom, in addition to other information. After obtaining this information, the officer will then turn on the lights and siren to signal that you are being pulled over. In some cases the officer could be behind you with blue lights and sirens on but you are not their target. It is not necessary to try to determine if you are the target or not. Just pull over. If the officer pulls in behind you, you are the target. If they continue on their way it wasn't your time. When I was on patrol I absolutely hated those people who tried to figure out if they were being pulled over. They would slow down look in their rear view mirrors and point at themselves as to say "Are you pulling me over?" The laws in most states are very specific. When emergency lights are behind your vehicle you must pull over to the right. If people would simply follow that simple law a driver would quickly find out if they were the unlucky driver being pulled over.

Now that the traffic stop has been initiated and the vehicle has been pulled over it is imperative that you remain calm. Remember, in some instances the officer may be more afraid of the driver than the driver is afraid of the officer. The officer has no idea what to expect from a driver so they sometimes might arrive prepared for the worst. If they do approach with a firm, focused and authoritative demeanor it is no reflection on you personally. To the officer, you represent an unknown and therefore could pose a threat to them. Because of the unknown element, the traffic stop is one of those necessary but dangerous parts of the job. As I stated before remain calm and keep a positive attitude.

The officer should advise you whether they want you to remain in the vehicle or step outside. If they ask you to remain in the vehicle, do so and refrain from reaching for anything or fidgeting. If they ask you to step out of the vehicle I would step out of the vehicle with my hands empty, refraining from placing my hands in my pockets unless I am directed to and then I would do so slowly. If I find myself speeding and pass an officer on the side of the road with a laser, my practice is to pull over immediately. Once my vehicle is stopped I let down both the driver window and front passenger window. I get my license from my front pocket because that is where I usually keep it. I have it ready when the officer approaches. I usually carry a small concealed handgun, which I keep on my hip, under my shirt and I generally do not mention that it is there. When the police ask you if you have a weapon you are not obligated to answer the question. Remember you have the right to remain silent, but use your own discretion with this. Sometimes when an officer knows a gun is present it tends to make them more nervous. I do my best to make the traffic stop a short encounter. If the officer approaches me and does not tell me why they stopped me I will ask why they stopped me. I do not argue with the officer. I hand them my license and let them be on their way. If it is dark outside, I turn on my interior lights and roll down the front windows. The illuminated vehicle assists the officer in seeing into the vehicle upon approach which assists the officer in observing the driver and passengers inside the vehicle. If the windows are tinted I roll down all of the windows and turn on the interior lights. I try to do what I can to make the officer's job easy by keeping them calm and at ease. This tends to expedite the encounter and in some cases prevents me from being issued a speeding citation.

There is nothing more important to an officer than people's hands during a traffic stop. The officer would probably feel more comfortable and at ease if they were able to see everyone's hands, not necessarily outside the window which would be more of a distraction than just keeping the hands unoccupied. Someone who has their hands outside a window or raised to the roof of the vehicle may grow tired and lower their hands causing the officer to become distracted with where the person's hands have gone and what they might be doing.

The officer will approach your vehicle either on the driver side or the passenger side. The passenger side approach is generally safer for the officer as it allows them to conduct the stop away from dangerous vehicular traffic. Also, because the driver is expecting the officer to approach on the driver side a passenger side approach allows the officer to observe the driver and the passengers before making contact.

Once the officer makes contact with you, do not interrupt them. Allow the officer to tell you why you are being pulled over. There are occasions when some officers attempt to get you to admit guilt prior to informing the driver of why they were stopped. This is accomplished by asking the driver, "Do you know why I pulled you over?" Another question is "Do you know how fast you were going?" These questions are sometimes meant to establish probable cause when the officer has none. A response of "No, I do not know" would be an appropriate response and in line with your Fifth Amendment Right against self-incrimination. Even if you know you were traveling 80 mph in a 55 mph zone the officer may not have known that. They may have pulled you over because your tag light was out. If asked, just say "No I do not know". If the officer does not tell you why they stopped you it is OK to ask them why they stopped you. Remember now is not the time to demand you get your respect. Your recourse for inappropriate or unprofessional behavior is a formal complaint. No matter how professional or unprofessional the officer may be you should always take the higher road by being polite and calm.

For the most part, all vehicle registration and insurance information is automated (officers can access the information by computer) which means the officer may not ask you for registration and insurance cards. They may only ask you for your license. If they do ask for a registration and or insurance card be cooperative and give it to them. It should be noted that you should always have an up to date insurance card in your vehicle at all times and a good rule to have a copy of the registration as well. In the past officers used the insurance card information to verify there was valid insurance coverage on the vehicle and to ensure the proper insurance information was recorded in the event of an accident. Likewise the registration card was used in the past to verify the correct tag was on the correct vehicle. (In the event of an accident the officer could easily obtain the vehicle identification number (VIN), tag number and registered owner information through the automated services.)

With technology upgrades to police vehicles and online information, officers rarely need insurance and registration cards any longer. All car insurance companies have automated their insurance information with Department of Motor Vehicle Services across the country, allowing the officer to input a vehicle tag number or VIN and get a return that includes the vehicle make, model, color, VIN, in some cases date of purchase, registered owner name and address, insurance carrier and policy number.

The officer will need the driver license of the person operating the vehicle. This is to ensure the driver is properly licensed and without license suspensions or revocations. Once the officer obtains the license of the driver they will then return to their vehicle and conduct a license check. The license check is conducted through the local state Crime Information Center and the National Crime Information Center in addition to the local Department of Driver Services. The check can yield information related to license validity, class and expiration, outstanding warrants, probation and parole information, terrorist watch lists and sexual offender status. It is important for the officer to know as much as possible about the people they are encountering especially those who have outstanding warrants.

Generally people who have outstanding warrants know they have these warrants and are not in jail because they didn't want to be there. An officer who stops someone who has an outstanding warrant and reluctant to go to jail can pose a threat to the officer. This warrant information should cause the officer to approach the driver or person being stopped with caution whereas without that information they might not use caution.

A sex offender alert could be important if the officer receives a return with a positive sex offender status and found the driver is accompanied by children. The information would alert the officer to ask questions of the person stopped and the child whereas without the information they normally would not have asked any questions .

Now that the officer has obtained information related to validity of the license, outstanding warrants, vehicle registration and other information, they are prepared to issue a citation. The officer will usually complete the citation in the vehicle; however, some find it safer to complete the citation on the side of the road. Some departments are still handwriting citations and other departments type in the information and print a neat, legible citation. After the officer has completed the citation he/she will return to your vehicle and inform you if they are issuing a citation or warning in addition to what the citation is for and the assigned court date. The officer will present you with a citation that *you must sign*. In Georgia, you sign the citation to acknowledge you are aware of your charge and the court date. The signature is the same as posting a bond. If you refuse to sign the citation you will be required to post a bond which means you will be arrested and taken to jail until you post a bond.

Outstanding Warrants

An outstanding warrant alert can put an officer on edge whether the warrant is for jaywalking or murder. If you become aware that you have an outstanding warrant take care of that warrant as soon as possible. Warrants can be issued for a number of reasons such as failure to pay child support, failure to appear for court, commission of a crime, etc. If you happen to have an outstanding warrant and you are stopped by the police be forthcoming and inform the officer ahead of time, remain calm, keep your hands visible and still. If they go back to the car and find out the vehicle operator has a warrant. The information may put the officer a little more on edge as they approach your vehicle. They may alert other officers to respond as backup. If you have a warrant, you have a warrant, take care of it and move on. It was not the fault of the officer that you decided not to pay traffic fines, violated your probation, or whatever it was that you did, and now isn't the time to dispute the warrant.

Anytime an officer is making an arrest should be a time for calm for the driver. Stay calm as you explain your situation. If the officer won't listen don't get upset. Officers listen to excuses and lies often and some have taken the stance to not listen to anything someone might have to say on a traffic stop. Regardless of their reaction say your piece but do not get upset if the officer does not respond the way you want them to or think they should. I am aware there have been innocent people arrested due to identity theft, improper identification on the part of an officer or miscommunication with the officer and a NCIC terminal operator, but trust me during an arrest is not the time to get upset and dispute the arrest. Remain calm! If they will not listen, ask for a supervisor. Remember stay calm. If the officer determines they need to place you in handcuffs to further investigate the issue stay calm and ask if you are under arrest. In some cases, officers place people in handcuffs to ensure a fight does not ensue or to prevent suspects from fleeing. I do not condone arresting innocent people nor do I condone placing people in handcuffs to figure things out or figure out what the charge will be. The time in which an officer is making a physical arrest (placing someone in handcuffs) can be one of the most dangerous times an officer faces in the performance of their duties. The officer is already on edge and playing several scenarios of how the encounter could end so just stay calm and make the encounter as positive as possible! I have seen both officers and citizens make an encounter much worse than it had to be simply because the person being arrested did not remain calm. It is important that the person being stopped remains calm. Being calm does not mean you are admitting you are guilty by not being loud and boisterous. There is no need to "save face" it isn't about the people watching the police put you in handcuffs so do not put on a show for them. It is not time to be filled with pride. It is time for a calm head. I cannot say this enough at times when I have been accused of doing something I did not do, I can get pretty angry but this is not the time, STAY CALM!

The End of the Traffic Stop

Once the officer issues you a citation, you sign it, return it and the officer gives you your copy, you are free to leave. The traffic stop is over! Again, some officers may use trickery to prolong the traffic stop. They will extend the stop by asking you to search your vehicle. Remember if they had probable cause to search your vehicle they would not have waited until after you had been given a citation and they certainly would not have asked you to search. Another ploy that is used is the threat to contact a K9 officer which would ensure a longer wait. Since most people value their time and are reluctant to spend more than necessary with the police they give the officer consent to search their vehicle. Officers get away with this because citizens are not aware they can leave. According to *Rodriguez v. United States*, during a traffic stop the officer can investigate the infraction in which they made the stop for but upon satisfying the tasks related to that infraction the stop is over. The officer cannot prolong the stop unless there is articulable reasonable suspicion that an additional crime is occurring or had occurred. The court was specific in saying the officer cannot prolong the stop for a K9 search. An example in which it would be appropriate to prolong a stop would be if the officer received prior knowledge that an armed robbery had occurred and the suspect was wearing a black mask. The same officer observed a vehicle fail to stop at a stop sign an hour after the robbery. The officer approached the vehicle, made contact with the driver, checked the drivers information, issued a citation and before walking away, she noticed a black mask in the back seat of the vehicle. The officer prolonged the traffic stop, creatively, by telling the driver they had issued the wrong court date on the citation and would have to issue a replacement. The officer asked for the license again and requested the driver wait until she returned. The officer contacted backup officers and detained the driver until an investigator arrived. These actions were within the law because the black mask created a reasonable suspicion that the driver may have been involved in the previously reported armed robbery. If the officer attempts to detain you any further after being given your copy of the citation ask calmly, "Am I free to leave at this time?" If the officer detains you any longer than the traffic stop, they must have probable cause or articulable reasonable suspicion to continue to detain you.

There have been occurrences in which an officer may "say" they smell marijuana. The courts have said due to an officers training and experience if they smell the odor of marijuana it is no different than a drug dog smelling marijuana. If the officer smells marijuana it gives them probable cause to search your vehicle. This is not a consent search. In these cases there is a possibility you rolled one a few weeks ago and there are some seeds on the floorboard. Some officers have been known to collect the seeds and charge you with possession of less than an ounce just so they have the justification for the search. Some jurisdictions have made possession of marijuana less than an ounce pretty much a nonevent but don't get caught in one of those jurisdictions where a little marijuana is considered a "big time drug arrest". If you have an odor of marijuana on your body and you are traveling in a vehicle and that vehicle gets pulled over be prepared for a vehicle search.

> **TIP:** Do not smoke marijuana and drive! Do not get into a vehicle if you smell like marijuana, unless it is legal in your jurisdiction.

Many people believe they have the "right" to refuse to sign a traffic citation. I believe it is important to go over this again. You do not have to sign the citation but if you do not sign the citation you must post a bond! In order to post a bond you have to be arrested. Signing the citation is not saying you are guilty but indicates you are aware of what you are being cited for and what your court date is. You are signing the citation *in lieu of posting a bond*. This is written at the bottom of the citation but some officers may not explain it to you. After refusing to sign the citation the next thing you know you are being asked to step out of the vehicle and to place your hands behind your back. I can only imagine that an officer would do this for someone who was less than polite and cooperative. Your citation should have the date that you are to appear in court; however, often, you have the option to pay the fine prior to the court date. If you choose to go to court, know the law. Have something substantial to offer other than, "I did not do what the officer said," because I guarantee you, if the officer does show up and that is all you have you probably wasted the day. Now, the officer showing up for court is another issue all together. In some jurisdictions this is a huge problem. The officers write the citations but then they do not show up for court. Sometimes the case is rescheduled so the officer can be there but in some jurisdictions the judges simply dismiss the case. If you are weighing a $25 dollar court cost (for example) versus a $400 fine, I would probably go to court just in case the officer does not show up. If the case is dismissed you could save $425.

Personal Anecdote: *While on patrol I sat in a sweet spot, watching an intersection for red light violators. I saw a vehicle fail to stop at a red light. I pulled the driver over and told him why he was being stopped. I issued him a citation for failure to obey a traffic control device. I have done this numerous times at this same intersection. Some people went to court and some just paid the fine. When I went to court with this guy, he asked for a trial. His defense was the light had previously malfunctioned. He had documentation of each malfunction. The judge threw out the ticket and said the light was not dependable. I had never had that happen before. So, either this guy was some type of engineer, had first-hand knowledge of the traffic lights, knew the impact of a malfunction, or someone told him it was a good defense. Either way, I had to shake that man's hand and tell him good job. Not only was I beat, but he gave me another secret to give to you. If you get a failure to stop at a red light ticket, do an open records request for repairs* *made to the traffic light. If there were repairs and you can prove the light had a history of malfunctioning then you MAY get out of the ticket.* The reason I say MAY get out of the ticket is because it all depends on the judge. The judge who ruled on that case was a defense attorney and had the mindset that the police should make strong cases. If the cases were not strong cases backed by evidence, she oftentimes ruled for the offender. The judge before her was quite the opposite. Whatever the police officer said happened was the truth as far as the judge was concerned. It was truly the offender's word against the officer's word, and the officer always won.

Passengers

If you are travelling with passengers have a conversation ahead of time. Tell them if you get pulled over not to say a word and don't do anything. Have the rear and front passenger put their hands in their laps (never the pockets), remain calm and allow you to handle the officer. The officer should not address your passengers unless they either feel threatened or they have noticed a violation. Remember, once the officer gets behind you they are observing everything that is done inside the vehicle. They can see people reaching for items, reaching underneath seats and other movements inside the vehicle. If you are reaching, the officer might interpret the movement as an attempt to hide something. Do not give the officer any reason to become alarmed.

I offer these suggestions for you and your passengers:
- Do not drink and drive. If your passengers are drinking all of you could be charged with having an open container.
- Do not drive under the influence of narcotics or travel with narcotics in your vehicle.
- If you have a firearm, the Supreme Court ruled your car is an extension of your home; thus you can travel with your weapon unless you are a convicted felon and that is a whole other issue.
- Basic rule of thumb when allowing others to travel with you know them very well and keep them in check if stopped by the police.

Infractions

There are several traffic related infractions that will get a driver stopped and most likely cited. I have listed some of the most common traffic infractions and tips on how to avoid being stopped for violating them.

When it comes to speeding, I have a severe need for speed. I know it comes from racing from call to call at least that's what I tell myself. Here are some secrets I still use when I'm travelling: Watch the people in front of you. It is a natural instinct to hit the brakes when you see a police officer whether you are speeding or not. If the people in front of you are braking you need to slow down—there is probably a police officer in the area. Police officers who write speeding tickets usually use a laser rather than the old radar. They can hit your car with a laser beam over 2400 feet away coming towards them and going away from them. This means they see you before you see them. It is possible that they have clocked you at 15 miles per hour over the speed limit before you even know they are there. Just because you slowed to the speed limit when you saw them don't argue that you weren't speeding. The officer is looking through a viewer, similar to binoculars, they point the laser right at the front or rear bumper of a particular car (depending on whether they are traveling towards you or away from you). They usually point at the leading car or a car they see closing in fast on the leading car. I haven't figured or heard a way to beat it other than abstinence. Just don't speed.

Police officers generally do not write tickets in the rain but then it is probably a bit too dangerous to speed at that time anyway. The traffic officers usually hide off the roadway a bit. They can be in cars or on motorcycles. If you are travelling on the interstate the officers are usually parked under an overpass or along the shoulder. They often find places in the grassy areas along the interstate. The officers try to hide their vehicle in plain sight. The car will usually be parked backed into a place with the front bumper facing the roadway. They sometimes sit with all their lights off so you can't see them or they sit with all their lights on so you can see them. When an officer is parked in plain sight they are generally there to deter speeding by their presence or taking a break. If you see the laser gun being pointed they are actively enforcing speeding laws.

Personal Anecdotes: *When going to work, I sometimes took a state route that had a long hill you had to travel until you came to a traffic light. When you reached the traffic light there were four to six uniform motorcycle officers waiting to write tickets. They pointed their lasers at vehicles just as they hit the top of the hill. By the time the vehicles reached the traffic light, it was too late. After I saw that once I always slowed down before I reached the hill, then looked to the sidewalk at the bottom of the hill to see if the officers were present. So, pay attention. If you see the police with a speed trap once, know that it is probable that they will be back at some point.*

I was traveling to Meridian, Mississippi for a training class. Just past the Mississippi state line, I observed about 10 police officers standing on the bridge, all with lasers. Along the side of the interstate there were marked police vehicles lined up ready to catch violators. I had never seen anything like this before, but I can assure you it made me slow down.

Small towns in between tourist destinations are notorious for their speed traps. If you are travelling by car take some time and do a little research on your route. Beware of the speed traps. There are cellphone applications that can assist you with locating police activity.

At every intersection there is either a stop sign or a traffic light. At these intersections there are white stop lines called stop bars, painted on the ground. If your vehicle rolls past the stop bar you have failed to stop at the stop sign or traffic light. Generally when this citation is written it is usually due to the vehicle not coming to a complete stop. Failure to come to a complete stop or more commonly called a "California stop" is no different than just driving through the intersection. In some jurisdictions the law is so specific it may say all four tires have to come to a complete stop. Yes, there are officers who watch stop signs and wait for us to roll right through. The next time you roll up to that stop sign make sure your vehicle comes to a complete stop at the stop bar. When vehicles are in front of us and they stop at the stop sign we sometimes look both ways as we are stopped behind the car. When that vehicle pulls away from the stop sign we pull away as well because we have already checked to see if there is traffic approaching. But what you are really doing is a rolling stop because your vehicle never came to a complete stop at the stop bar. Your vehicle came to a complete stop behind the vehicle that was behind the stop bar. So, pull to the stop sign, which should be adjacent to the stop bar and come to a complete stop. Remember whether you stop or not, it will boil down to your word against the officer's and the odds that you would be believed over the officer without evidence, is slim to none. Rarely does an officer utilize video to capture the vehicle failing to stop.

Intersections that are controlled by traffic lights are generally larger than those controlled by a stop sign. I have seen some pretty horrific traffic accidents in my career and most of them resulted from someone failing to stop at a red light. Traffic lights and the disobedience of the yellow caution and red stoplights create a dangerous situation. The inability to wait for a few minutes for the light to turn green can and have cost people their lives. When approaching a yellow light it does not mean speed up to get through before the light turns red. It means slow down, cautiously approach the intersection, and prepare to stop. Failure to stop at a traffic light generally means that you have crossed the stop bar when the light was red. Generally, if your vehicle is in the intersection before the light turns red you might be considered safe. Again, just as with the stop sign, it is your word against the officers, and I'm not going to wager with those odds. My advice to you is slow down as you approach the intersection and prepare to stop which is really what the yellow light means.

This is a good time for me to mention emergency lights and sirens here. If you hear them in the area look and ensure it is not on your right and then pull to the right making a lane of traffic for the emergency vehicle. There is nothing like trying to get through traffic with lights and sirens and people just look at you behind them. *Get out of the way*! That officer might be responding to an armed robbery in which someone you know has a gun pointed to their head. You just never know, so **get out of the way!**

Personal Anecdote: *Now, there was that time I was in a patrol vehicle in which the lights would come on by themselves. So, I was just cruising around with my lights going. I had no idea until I stopped in a parking lot to do a report and heard the lights on (they make a slight ticking sound when they are activated). I have also seen other officers riding around with lights going, while I'm in my personal vehicle. I pull up to them and tell them, but my spouse says that's not safe. So, if you decide to tell them their lights are going, while they are sitting at a red light, be safe doing it. You can usually tell when they don't know the lights are going, because they aren't in a hurry, they appear relaxed, and they are obeying all traffic laws.*

Another traffic infraction that gets a lot of people stopped is the no turn on red violation. When a vehicle approaches an intersection, especially when making a right turn, do not just look for other cars in the intersection look for signs. Look on the side of the road as you approach the intersection, look on the traffic light fixtures, look all around the intersection. These signs hide in plain sight and blend in well with other signs. Officers hide in parking lots to watch these intersections. They know you aren't looking for those signs. It is engrained in our heads that you can turn right on a red light so why do we need to look for a sign? We don't even think about it as we approach the intersection. Think about turning right on red and look for those signs before you turn.

An officer who is looking for a reason to pull over a vehicle will sometimes follow the vehicle until an infraction is observed.

When a driver views a police officer in the rear view mirror it will make any person nervous. Nervousness can make a driver slow down and drive in a deliberate manner in which every move is thought out prior to. On the other hand a driver becomes nervous and begins to drive erratically. Infractions that are common in this instance are failing to maintain lane. A simple maneuver over the center line or over the dashed white line can get a driver pulled over.

A second nervousness infraction is failing to signal a lane change or turn. This action should be a habit for everyone but it isn't. We should always signal to let the other drivers know what we intend to do. Whether we are turning right or left, it is good to communicate this to everyone else allowing them to know what our intentions are so we can minimize the chances for an accident. It has been my experience that this citation is rarely written unless the failure to signal caused an accident. The officer does not have to be behind you to know you didn't signal. If you get into the practice of signaling the chances that you will signal when you are being followed by a police officer will increase drastically.

Equipment violations are also infractions that can get a driver pulled over. These infractions are also used by drug interdiction officers as probable cause to make traffic stops that lead to drug investigations. The headlights on a vehicle are expected to be operable when visibility is low. For example, in Georgia, when it is raining, the headlights are expected to be on, in addition to being on at dusk and at dawn. This is one of those rules where the headlight requirement is not cited unless there is an accident or the officer is looking for a reason to pull you over. The tag light, which is something you probably never thought about, is located right above your rear license plate. Again, officers hardly ever even think to look at this light unless they are in need of a reason to pull you over. A good rule of thumb is to always do a little inspection of your vehicle before driving. Make sure all of your lights are operable and your license plate is displayed properly, which means it is in the correct place and there is nothing covering the decal (the year sticker). A few years ago that was a big thing—the license plate holders or frames you buy to put around your license plate didn't have the cutouts so the decals could be displayed. Officers used this as a reason to pull vehicles over. Now they are designed to properly display the decals. Speaking of decals, did you know the color of the decal indicates the year of expiration? For example, when I renewed my vehicle registration I was issued a decal with the year 2014 on it. Let's say 2014 is a white decal. I placed the white decal over an orange decal. The colors are to differentiate the expiration years. Officers use the colors to determine whether your registration might be expired. It is much easier to see the colors rather than that year in such small print. They also have those handy in car computers that they use to determine what the actual date of expiration is. You should be familiar with your state law related to the vehicle registration expiration. In some jurisdictions the registration expires on your birthday and in others it expires at the end of your birth month.

Who would have thought bald tires and cracked windshields could get you pulled over? I know this may seem like a joke but bald tires can get you pulled over. Your tires have to have a predetermined depth of tread on the tires. This requirement is a safety precaution that must be acknowledged. The depth of the tread prevents vehicular accidents especially during inclement weather.

There is also a law prohibiting windshield cracks of the spider web or starburst effect greater than three inches by three inches. This, too, is a safety requirement that must be acknowledged. A large spider web type crack can impair the drivers field of view causing a risk for accidents. Again, these are laws that are enforced in the event of an accident or used as probable cause to stop a vehicle (just a reason to pull you over).

It is common for some officers to utilize stops for minor infractions like equipment violations to pull drivers over. These type of stops are primarily used in drug interdiction. An officer may see a vehicle leaving a known drug area (place where drugs are known to be sold and or consumed) and proceed to follow that vehicle looking for an infraction to pull it over. At some point the officer is going to ask for permission to search the vehicle. They may believe you have purchased drugs or sold drugs but there is no evidence of such a transaction meaning no probable cause to pull the vehicle over for a drug related crime. However there is probable cause to pull the vehicle over for the equipment violation. Officers use these types of laws to pull you over for an investigatory stop. During an **investigatory stop** they are "supposed" to investigate the reason they stopped you but in some cases it is used to investigate the reason they "really" stopped you. It should be noted as previously stated the officer cannot detain you any longer than it takes to satisfy the requirements for the violation they stopped you for.

Let's just say, for instance, you are driving a white BMW 750 and your vehicle is seen leaving an area where drugs are known to be sold. The officer wants to pull you over because they believe you might have something to do with the drugs, either purchasing, selling, or distributing. That is the "real" reason they want to pull you over. However, as they pass your vehicle they notice a crack in the windshield, or a tag light out, or the tread on the tire doesn't look so deep. It could be a number of small infractions. But those small infractions are golden to the police because they give the officers the probable cause they need to pull you over. After they pull you over "supposedly" to investigate the crack in the windshield, they begin to ask you other questions, like, "Where are you going? Where are you coming from? Can I search your vehicle?" These things have nothing to do with the crack in your windshield.

I know you are thinking the officer is profiling you. However, if the officer has a legitimate reason to pull you over, no matter how insignificant you think the violation is, is it profiling or are they just doing their jobs to protect and serve? That answer is argued daily. The point here is to prepare yourself, prepare your passengers, and prepare your vehicle. If they don't have a reason to stop you then they should not stop you or it may be considered profiling. If this happens to you write a formal complaint.

> **TIP:** *You do not have to let the police search your vehicle unless they have probable cause or a warrant. If you do allow the police to search your vehicle, you have the right to tell them to stop at anytime! If the police asked me to search my vehicle, I would ask this: "so, you are asking my consent to search my vehicle and I can take that consent away at any time? Is that what you are saying?" The point is you want to confirm that they are indeed asking for your consent to search and confirming that you can take that consent away at any time. That is your right! The traffic stop is over once you sign the citation and they give you your copy!*

Driving Under the Influence

I do not condone driving under the influence but I included this section so the average citizen would know what to expect. The charge of driving under the influence, depending on what state you are located in, could be referred to as driving while intoxicated (DWI), drunk driving, or driving while impaired. There are two different categories of being under the influence: alcohol or drugs. As discussed previously the officer has to have probable cause to pull you over. This probable cause could be weaving in your lane (driving from side to side), failure to maintain your lane (traveling over the center line or the dashed line designating your lane of travel), the result of an accident or many other infractions. From the point the officer observed you violate the rules of the road (the law); they are constantly observing you to gather more probable cause.

You can look at the DUI stop as building a structure. The foundation was the reason they stopped you and it has to be solid. Then the officer makes every attempt to place solid blocks on top of the foundation to build the case. As they approach the vehicle they are watching you. When they get to your window they will have their nostrils wide open attempting to detect the slightest aroma of an alcoholic beverage or drugs. They will ask you questions to get you to speak which causes the smell of an alcoholic beverage to emit from your breath. Such questions include, "Do you know why I stopped you?" This also presents an opportunity to hear your speech. If your speech is slurred that is another building block to the DUI case. They will ask you for your license and watch you remove it from your wallet or pocket. They are observing your dexterity and ability to concentrate on simple tasks.

Once the officer obtains your license they may hang around and ask more questions, like: "Have you been drinking tonight? When was the last time you had a drink? Have you been smoking marijuana? or, When was the last time you were smoking marijuana?" Remember it is your right to remain silent. You do not have to announce to the officer that you have this right just be quiet. They will run your license to make sure it is valid (meaning it is not suspended or revoked) and also to determine if you have any outstanding warrants. Anything you say *will* be used against you later.

The next step in the DUI investigation is the field sobriety evaluations. These laws vary in different states so be informed. In Georgia, a driver is not obligated to take the roadside evaluations. Your refusal means they cannot use the results against you (no building block.) They may tell you that you are going to be placed under arrest for suspicion of driving under the influence or driving less safe. They will transport you and put you in front of their intoxilyzer which is a breath test machine (some jurisdictions do this test on the scene). This machine measures the amount of alcohol in a person's breath. Only a blood sample can provide accurate blood alcohol content (BAC). In Georgia, before they take you away, they have to read you the implied consent card. Basically this is just to remind you that *since you are a licensed driver in Georgia you must agree to give a sample of your blood, breath or urine (the officer's choice).*

****Note the breath test is the least expensive and fastest option****

A driver can refuse to take the breath test. *A person's refusal to take the breath test will result in the immediate suspension of their license.* When a driver refuses the test (this means no building block) the officer will obtain your license and provide you with a hearing date where you can request a driving permit and appeal the suspension of your license. This will allow you to drive back and forth to work. Now, if you are caught leaving a nightclub and you do not work there you may be arrested for driving with a suspended license.

Suspended License

Depending on the laws in your local jurisdiction a driver's license can be suspended or revoked for a number of violations including but not limited to: mandatory suspensions, common suspensions, under the age of 21 suspensions, and suspensions due to the use, possession, sale or distribution of controlled substances or marijuana (dds.Georgia.gov).

Mandatory Suspensions include homicide by vehicle, any felony in the commission of which a motor vehicle is used, using a motor vehicle in fleeing or attempting to elude an officer, fraudulent application for a license or fictitious use of a license, hit and run, leaving the scene of an accident, racing, operating a motor vehicle with a revoked, canceled, or suspended registration, and felony forgery relating to an identification document.

Common Suspensions include refusal to take a chemical test in conjunction with an arrest for DUI, conviction for driving without insurance, if convicted for driving while license is suspended, the driver's license will be further suspended for six months, failure to pay child support, failure to appear in court or respond to a traffic citation may result in your license being suspended indefinitely, any violation of the Georgia Control Substance Act, DDS is authorized to suspend your license if its records or other evidence shows that you have accumulated 15 points within 24 months under the point system, including violations committed out of state.

Under the age of 21 Suspensions include hit and run or leaving the scene of an accident, racing on highways or streets, using a motor vehicle in fleeing or attempting to elude an officer, reckless driving, any offense for which four or more points are assessable. (A)Unlawful passing of a school bus. (B) Improper passing on a hill or curve. (C) Exceeding the speed limit by 24 miles per hour or more. (D) Aggressive Driving, purchasing an alcoholic beverage, driving under the Influence, misrepresenting age for purpose of illegally obtaining any alcoholic beverage, misrepresenting identity or using false identification for purpose of purchasing or obtaining any alcoholic beverage, the driver's license of any person under 18 years of age who has accumulated a violation point count of four or more points within any 12 month period.

Use, possession, sale or distribution of controlled substances or marijuana-A person convicted of possession, distribution, sale, use, etc., of a controlled substance or marijuana will be subject to the suspension of his or her driver's license or driving privilege even if the offense did not occur in or involve the use of a motor vehicle.

Driving on a suspended license can result in being arrested and taken to jail to post a bond. Some states have invested in websites that will allow you to check the status of your license. If your license is not valid, you should immediately contact your state driver services office to fix the situation.

8
OTHER NOTEABLE OFFENSES

Rule 8: *Knowing "catch all" charges can help citizens avoid being investigated and charged, limiting negative interactions.*

There are many other infractions or criminal charges that an officer can charge a person with. Some of these charges are designed to be all encompassing. An example would be disorderly conduct. This law describes multiple behaviors that are considered criminal. I refer to these type of laws as "catch all" charges. "Catch all" charges are real crimes but in some cases they are used by some officers when they have placed people under arrest but then they realize that the behavior the citizen may have displayed does not match the elements of the crime the officer thought they could have charged the citizen with. Rather than just letting the citizen go and admitting to a mistake they charge the person with one of those "catch all" charges. Examples include obstruction and disorderly conduct. The following pages explain several notable laws.

Failure to leave schools and universities

- For the sake of this section these schools and universities are limited to those that receive public funds.
- When you are not a student, employee or required to be on campus and you are asked to leave by the administration or their designee (usually a police or

security officer) you must leave or you can be arrested for disorderly conduct

- When an employee, administrator or their designee (usually a police or security officer) reasonably believes that a person is *likely* to interfere with peaceful conduct on campus they can be asked to leave.

You can be asked to leave for any reason the officer believes may disrupt the peace. (An example of a disruption would be a parent becoming irate and belligerent during a parent conference.) If the administrator asks a disruptive parent to leave (it doesn't matter whether you as the parent believe you are disruptive) you MUST leave or you can be arrested for failure to leave when directed. If you are attending a school sponsored event and the administration believes you or your group are likely to cause a disturbance they can ask you to leave. This is important for parents and students to know.

Giving a false name to officers- Giving a law enforcement officer, who is performing official duties, a false name, address or date of birth in an attempt to mislead the officer is against the law. In conducting field investigations it is often necessary to ask your name, address and date of birth. The information is then checked with state and national databases to ensure that you are who you say you are and that the officer is not speaking with someone who has outstanding warrants. To help with all of this just carry an identification card. If you give the officer a name, date of birth and/or address other than your true name date of birth and/or address you can be placed under arrest.

Personal Anecdote: *After receiving a complaint of people loitering on a corner selling drugs I arrived and approached a group of people, asked for identifications and began to check the names with the databases. While the checks were being conducted I asked if the people lived in the area and they did not. One of the males gave me the name and date of birth of his brother, who was currently incarcerated. (I knew he was incarcerated because my group had recently completed the court case that he was sentenced for.) Based on the information from the data base, the person who gave us his brother's name had an outstanding warrant for failure to appear. He was arrested for giving the false information and the outstanding warrant.*

False Report of a Crime- Any person who makes a false report to a law enforcement officer or a law enforcement agency can be arrested. During the course of my career I have taken many types of reports. In some cases those reports were false. Either the act never happened or it did not happen like it was reported. Maybe in the past it was easy to make these reports of thefts and assaults but now with a camera almost everywhere it has become easier for law enforcement to follow-up on these reports. People have made false reports for a number of reasons but the point here is not to do it because you can be arrested for it. Law enforcement agencies talk to each other so if you try to make a report at one agency and they tell you no for whatever reason do not change the circumstances and attempt to make the report at another agency because if it is proven that what you reported is not true you can be arrested.

Personal Anecdote: *Many years ago I was investigating a burglary that occurred around the first of the month. The victim reported $975 in cash was taken from her bedroom nightstand drawer. The entire apartment was in disarray and the back door appeared to be damaged. I won't go into how the case was solved but this was a case of a false report of a crime. The rent was due but had been spent on other things.*

Interference with 911- If someone verbally or physically prevents someone from making an emergency call with the intent to cause or allow physical harm, it is against the law. You can be arrested. An example here is if during an altercation a victim decides to call 911 and the perpetrator rips a phone cord out of the wall causing the call to be disconnected or takes a cellphone from the victim's hands and disconnects the call or verbally hinders the victim from continuing a 911 call by making threats of physical harm, placing the victim in fear of their life may cause the perpetrator to be arrested and charged with interference with 911. This charge is often used in incidents involving family violence.

Disorderly conduct

These laws have been challenged and modified in a number of jurisdictions. They are sometimes referred to as one of the "catch all" charges used by police. I will attempt to explain how these charges are used so that you can avoid being arrested for them. I have included the statute from Georgia, but other states include vague language within their codes and describe a wide array of behaviors that are illegal under those statutes. For example, in New York the disorderly conduct law describes the following actions as illegal: fighting, unreasonable noise, using abusive language or gestures in public, disturbing a meeting or gathering, obstructing vehicular or pedestrian traffic, congregating with others and refusing to leave when ordered to do so, and a very vague creating a hazardous or physically offensive condition by any act which serves no legitimate purpose. In California one can be arrested for disorderly conduct for being under the influence of alcohol and or drugs, loitering, panhandling, etc. The Ohio and Alabama statutes appear to match New York verbatim.

In Georgia the code section reads (a) a person commits the offense of disorderly conduct when such a person commits any of the following:
(1) Acts in a violent or tumultuous manner toward another person whereby such person is placed in reasonable fear of the safety of such person's life, limb or health;

(2) Acts in a violent tumultuous manner toward another person whereby the property of such person is placed in danger of being damaged or destroyed;

(3) Without provocation, uses to or of another person in such other person's presence, opprobrious or abusive words which by their very utterance tend to incite to an immediate breach of the peace, that is to say, words which as a matter of common knowledge and under ordinary circumstances will, when used to or of another person in such other person's presence, naturally tend to provoke violent resentment, that is words commonly called "fighting words"; or

(4) Without provocation, uses obscene and vulgar or profane language in the presence of or by telephone to a person under the age of 14 years which threatens an immediate breach of the peace (O.C.G.A. 16-11-39).

Each of these states have enacted disorderly conduct statutes that appear to be similar; however, you should also realize that counties and cities have the authority to expand the law into more detailed, unlawful behavior. For example, it may be unlawful to walk in the street when there is a sidewalk available. If a police officer stops someone for this violation of law it is not racial profiling it is an officer enforcing the laws. The problem lies when these laws are not enforced across the board but only in certain communities. If it is a traffic hazard in a one community it is a traffic hazard in every community. I think it is important to understand these laws and the behaviors they describe to avoid being approached by police. In most of the instances in which I observed violations of these disorderly conduct laws I approached the suspect and asked them to discontinue the behavior. The next step was to ask for an ID because if I had to spend more time with the suspect I would like to know who I was interacting with. I then checked their information to determine if I was speaking with someone who had an outstanding warrant. Usually by this time the suspect has thought about the consequences of continued interaction and decides to comply with my original request. Unfortunately some people just do not get it and wish to continue the interaction by not complying, which will most likely result in an arrest. What I fail to understand, even after 17 years is why people refuse to comply with the requests of the police. There are people who know they are doing something wrong but when stopped by the police they insist the officer prove their behavior was unlawful. The police officer is required to have probable cause to make an arrest not to **prove** the behavior was unlawful. In criminal cases judges and juries determine guilt or innocence. Officers issue suspects a court date, so they will have the opportunity to **argue** their case in front of a judge or jury. In the example given with disorderly conduct, if the suspect disagrees with why they are being stopped, they should not make a big deal out of it by arguing their point. They should just leave. If you have a complaint that the officer did something wrong, violated your rights or was unprofessional follow the procedures to make a written complaint. This section is very important and intended to encourage people to research what behaviors are illegal in their community to avoid these interactions with law enforcement. **Loitering or prowling** is often used for people hanging out but the law is very specific in stating what behaviors must be present to be loitering:

- A person is in a place at a time or in a manner not usual for law abiding individuals
- Being in that place at that time warrants a justifiable and reasonable alarm or immediate concern for the safety of persons or property in the area.
- In addition to the time and place the flight of the suspect when the see an officer can also be used to determine if there was justifiable and reasonable alarm
- If the suspect refuses to identify themselves or attempts to hide or conceal themselves
- Unless it is impractical the officer shall allow the suspect to dispel any alarm or immediate concern.

Basically, what this means to me, is if someone is in a place at a time that is not usual for law abiding people, the officer has a duty to stop the person and conduct a short interview to determine why they are there. If the person runs after seeing a police officer the officer has the duty to give chase and allow the person to explain why they were in the place at that time. If the explanation doesn't make sense to the officer or does not dispel the alarm the person caused they can be arrested. Walking behind closed businesses late at night, standing outside homes during the daytime hours when people are usually at work, walking through parking lots when you don't have a vehicle are some examples of situations in which an officer can stop you for suspicion of loitering and prowling.

When I try to determine if news stories about police officers and their patrol practices are fair or not I often think what if that happened in my mother's neighborhood. For example, if there was someone who did not live in my mom's neighborhood but was hanging out standing on a corner talking on the phone when everyone was at work I would not have a problem with a police officer stopping them to find out who they were and why they were there. Notice I did not say arrest the person for loitering but simply find out why they were there and request they move on. It would not matter what race or age they were I would rather be safe than have my mom or her neighbors have to report a burglary or worse. I have seen burglars work in pairs or groups with one standing on a corner as a look out while others in the group burglarize homes. This hanging out behavior is behavior that a trained patrol officer would question but a normal citizen probably wouldn't think twice about it. Usually this police intervention is enough to encourage the person to move on.

Obstruction

Emergency personnel and first responders have sometimes taken the brunt of citizens' traumatic situations. There have been instances in which emergency personnel and first responders are hindered from performing their duties. Because of this, in several jurisdictions there are laws that prohibit obstructing emergency personnel and first responders from performing their duties.

If someone knowingly and willfully obstructs or hinders a law enforcement officer, who is lawfully doing their job, that person can be arrested. Prison guards, correctional officers, probation supervisors, parole supervisors and conservation rangers can all be included when referring to obstruction of a law enforcement officer. Some consider this a "catch all" because it is so vague. A citizen should always be aware of their behavior when around officers who are conducting their official duties. This is why I repeated, so many times, when dealing with the police remain calm and tell your friends to remain calm. For example, if the police pull you over and the officer is attempting to investigate the traffic infraction by conducting an interview with the driver and a passenger continues to loudly interrupt to the point the officer is unable to perform his/her duties the passenger can be arrested. Anytime someone interferes with an officer doing their job no matter how minimal you believe your interference was you can be arrested. So my advice to you is if you see what you think is misconduct by an officer do not record at a distance where you can be considered interfering or a danger to the officer. Move away from the officer to record the incident, preferably across the street. **Something to remember-** In my opinion it is the officer's perception that determines whether they are in danger.

9
FAMILY VIOLENCE

Rule #9: *Knowing what family violence is can deter citizens from engaging in those behaviors that would place them in jeopardy of being involved in family violence incidents, limiting encounters with law enforcement.*

Domestic violence has evolved throughout the years from domestic violence to family violence but there has also been an increased focus on intimate partner abuse. All of these names have one thing in common and that is ABUSE. For the purpose of consistency we will refer to those incidents that involve family or couples who share children as family violence. Intimate partner abuse is generally reserved for dating couples who do not live together or share children.

Typically when we hear the phrase family violence, we immediately think husband/wife or male/female relationship, but there are so many other types of relationships that are included in Family Violence Laws. Some relationships include: past or present spouses, any parent/child relationship including birth parents, step parents, and foster parents, or any other people who have formerly or are currently sharing the same residence as recognized relationships. Same sex couples who are living together, domestic partners, married and (or) sharing children also fall under family violence laws.

Although not all victims of family violence and intimate partner abuse are female, female victims have sometimes been victimized by the perpetrator and then again by responding officers. The law enforcement response to family violence and intimate partner abuse has evolved over the years. Officers are held accountable for their response and required by law, in most jurisdictions, to take action. In the past officers responded to a call of assistance from a female with a threat "If we have to come back somebody is going to jail." This action would usually garner the requested response and no further calls would be made to police. The perpetrator, usually a male, might beat the victim or threaten to cause bodily harm to the victim if another call was made. In essence the victim was threatened by both the police and the perpetrator if there was another call made. Today laws are more clear and provide more instruction to officers in their response. In most jurisdictions officers are charged with identifying the primary aggressor of the altercation. The primary aggressor is usually the person who started the incident. In Georgia, officers are encouraged to determine the primary aggressor and place them under arrest if there is evidence that a crime has occurred. Evidence includes but is not limited to bruises, scratches, burns, broken windows, broken tables and holes in the wall. Basically any visible injury or property damage. If John pushed Stacey and Stacey pushed John back and there is no evidence or witness that there was a push from John he probably would not be arrested. There should be an attempt to separate the two parties for a while to calm the situation but this should not replace an effective investigation to determine who the primary aggressor is.

Family violence calls were some of the most difficult calls to handle for a number of reasons. First, they are very unpredictable such as when victims "change their minds" about reporting incidents that might potentially take a breadwinner from the home. A second reason these calls are difficult is due to personal biases regarding sexual orientation which can be a barrier for officers responding to family violence and intimate partner abuse calls. Another reason that makes these calls difficult is the potential danger they pose to responding officers. Lastly, obtaining facts relevant to the case can make responding to the call difficult when the call is made from someone who was not an involved party.

While on patrol early in my career, I responded to a call in which a victim contacted police and then changed their mind after the police arrived. The victim told the officers they changed their mind and did not want police assistance. When the officers attempted to investigate the call to ensure everything was ok the victim became combative. Victims sometimes change their minds about police assistance as a result of pressure from the suspect. They may feel guilty, especially if the suspect is in danger of being arrested. A change of mind can also result from a feeling of helplessness if the suspect is the breadwinner and has to go to jail, causing a lapse in financial benefits. There might also be negative feelings about the victim from children, siblings, in-laws, friends, etc. A large reason for the change in family violence laws was to remove that stigma from victims and place the burden of the arrest on the state (police officers) rather than the victim. The decision to arrest is the officers and not the victim. A change of mind cannot and should not determine the outcome of these incidents any longer.

I found responding to family violence incidents involving same sex couples posed a problem for most officers. It was difficult for them to move past their own biases and handle the calls just as they had handled calls involving heterosexual couples. Officers responded to a call in reference to a person armed with a knife. When the officers arrived it was determined the perpetrator and suspect were domestic partners and living in the same residence. The knife described was located at the scene and there was evidence that a physical altercation had occurred. The responding officer refused to place the perpetrator under arrest because he believed he would contract AIDS by touching the gay perpetrator. The perpetrator was allowed to leave the scene to "cool off". Response to incidents involving LGBTQ citizens has improved as a result of training and the hiring of more LGBTQ police officers. Some departments have LGBTQ liaisons to ensure there are open lines of communications between the LGBTQ community and law enforcement.

Responding to family violence and intimate partner abuse can oftentimes be a dangerous task for officers. In instances in which there is evidence of an assault to the victim or property damage in the presence of the victim there is usually an arrest made. The reluctance of someone to be arrested can cause them to resist that arrest which results in an altercation between the officer and the suspect. Generally when there is a repeat offender of family violence there may be an increased chance the offender will put up a fight rather than be arrested peacefully. Generally placing someone in handcuffs poses a great danger to the officers. In a family violence situation the officer not only has to be concerned with resistance from the perpetrator but also from the victim which is why these calls can be one of the most dangerous calls an officer will respond to. Officers responding to a family violence incident parked their patrol vehicle in front of the victim's home. As soon as officers exited their patrol vehicles and began to approach the residence they were fired upon. The officers were caught off guard as there was no warning that the suspect was armed. Officers responding to family violence incidents now use a more tactical approach when approaching an incident location and should assume there are firearms within the home.

Family violence and intimate partner abuse calls are sometimes made by people (complainants) who are not associated with the incident such as neighbors, children and (or) family members not at the scene. While these complainants may hear an altercation and make an initial call they are sometimes not willing to get more involved than that. When contacting 911 complainants are not willing to leave identifying information such as name, address or phone number. In those cases in which the complainant is willing to speak with officers they can usually only tell the officer what they heard. When officers approach the alleged victim and suspect they sometimes deny an altercation took place and make up a story to justify anything the neighbor may have heard. Victims often contact family members or trusted friends who then contact law enforcement. While they are willing to provide their personal information the information they provide about an incident is sometimes hearsay and they are unable to provide the officer any first-hand information. Although the police will respond to investigate, without corroboration from the victim or a witness inside the home or evidence of a crime, the officer may be unable to make an arrest for family violence.

Although the investigation by the responding officer is difficult, they should not cut corners and minimize what may have occurred. The police response to family violence incidents may require more officers than any other type of disturbance because they are proven to be volatile and fluid situations. The officer should begin by separating the parties according to the number of officers who are present. It is unsafe for an officer to respond to this type of call for service alone and even more dangerous to separate people alone, because they would have no idea what the party they are not speaking with is doing. Just as in a traffic stop, empty hands are important. The officer may ask all parties to stand or sit in certain rooms. The officer will attempt to remove the parties from any visible weapons. If the officer asks the parties to sit, he/she may search the area they asked the people to sit in. This is to ensure there are no weapons that can harm the officers while they are conducting their investigation. People are more apt to tell the truth when there is no pressure from others listening. After all parties are separated the officers are then to ask questions that illicit detailed descriptions of the incident. They should then look around the incident location to determine if there is evidence of a crime. If there is evidence an arrest should be made and photographs should be taken to preserve the scene and any evidence contained within that scene.

Anytime an officer responds to this type of call for service, they are or should be on high alert as these calls have the potential to become deadly. If the police respond to your home, someone called, giving the police authority to be there. Be calm and provide your side of the story. Listen to the instructions that the officer gives you to make certain there is no confusion. If at any time, when dealing with a police officer, you feel disrespected, right now, at the scene, is not the time or place to express those feelings. First of all, you are already upset and emotional. We don't do our best thinking at this time. The best way to handle being disrespected is to provide a written complaint to the Office of Professional Standards or Internal Affairs.

The officer should not show any biases towards one party or the other. There should also be no predetermined victim. Throughout my career I have encountered both male and female victims. Responding officers should handle these calls equally regardless of the gender or sexual orientation of the involved parties. Although police officers, in general, have improved their handling of domestic violence calls, there is always room for more improvement.

During the course of my investigative career I have had the opportunity to interview a number of women and men who have suffered from domestic abuse by a partner. I have learned abuse can be perpetrated in a number of ways including emotional abuse, sexual abuse and physical abuse. Emotional abuse was described as being more subtle than physical or sexual abuse. The emotional abuse was more of a tool used to gain psychological control of a partner. Most believed their abuse began with demeaning jokes and put downs before any physical abuse occurred. Eventually their abusers were able to eat away their self-confidence, self-esteem and ultimately their self-worth which was replaced with dependence. The put downs and jokes would be followed and supported by the words "I love you" causing the victim to associate the demeaning and emotionally abusive behavior with love. The behavior in human abuse victims can be associated to the theory of classical conditioning. The unconditioned stimulus is being loved or rather the thought of being loved. The unconditioned response is a sense of belonging in addition to what appears to be care and concern from the abuser. Any behavior that is associated with the words "I love you" is thought to be acceptable behavior. For example, if an abuser struck a female in the face and followed that behavior with the words "I love you", some abuse victims might associate that assault as an act of affection and love. In my opinion it is the conditioning of the victim that continues to exacerbate the abuse and it also acts as a barrier to the victim seeking assistance. Love is something we all wish to feel. We have to do better to make it clear that love and violence do not go hand in hand. Abuse should not be expected and normalized behavior.

In the course of my daily duties I tend to look at things through a law enforcement lens. I see teenagers with their mates. A male tells his female mate "come here." She refuses and he grabs her coat and says in an angry voice, "I said come here." I have seen a female snatch her mate's phone from his hands and say, " You better not be texting a girl." Both of these actions, although initiated by both a male and a female, are possessive behaviors and can be an indication of an abusive partner. Married couples in which one party holds the purse strings and denies the other access to funds is a form of abuse. The party who holds the purse strings has "control" over the finances and the other is dependent and has to request funds when needed. Abusive behavior may be as subtle as asking who you are speaking to, driving by your home to see if your car is there, sneaking up on you at a function with family or friends, and suggesting you not hang out with certain people or do certain things. They might suggest more suitable clothing and shoes or tell you how they prefer you to wear your hair. Abuse tends to escalate as the relationship progresses. If your partner displays these types of possessive and controlling behaviors pay close attention as they are red flags. People rarely change their behaviors. If you have recently begun a relationship and your partner is displaying these types of behaviors you will not be able to change them. Only they can change themselves. Are you willing to risk your life that they will change?

Victims of domestic abuse often find themselves with difficulty leaving an abusive relationship due to children or lack of financial resources. There are programs to assist you just take the first step. As a victim of abuse you should know that *you* cannot change your abuser! If you find yourself in an abusive relationship seek assistance by calling the police at 911 and the National Domestic Violence Hotline at 1-800-799-7233. Your life *matters!* If you are dating someone who does not value you, who regularly puts you down, cracks on you, hits you, curses and disrespects you, you can do better!

I would like to end this section with a bit of good advice I have learned along the way. *When people SHOW YOU who they REALLY are, BELIEVE them the FIRST TIME.* In incidents of domestic, family, and intimate partner violence you may not get a second or third chance.

10
AFTER AN ARREST

Rule #10: *Knowing what is expected after an arrest can promote positive citizen/police interactions by helping the suspect and family members understand various steps in the process.*

Police Interrogation

Generally when an incident occurs a report is taken by uniformed, field officer. The report is then usually approved by a supervisor. Depending on the type of case and size of the department it may be assigned to an investigator. In some agencies a uniform field officer may follow up on simple cases like thefts and minor assaults while more complex cases like rapes and homicides will be assigned to an investigator. The investigator will gather evidence, interview victims, witnesses and suspects, obtain search and arrest warrants in addition to other technical tasks related to the investigation. Generally after an investigator is assigned a case by a supervisor they should make contact with the victim immediately or within the next 48 hours. This is usually spelled out in the department policies and procedures. If the investigator leaves you a message or leaves a card in your door, call them back immediately. If the investigator does not contact you, you should be proactive in contacting them. Your case depends on the investigator gathering the necessary information and exhausting all possible leads in a timely manner.

I am not a lawyer and thus, not qualified to give you legal advice, but I will tell you this, *if you are arrested, you have the right to remain SILENT.* When the police stop you, they do not have to advise you of your right to silence or your right to have an attorney present when you are being questioned, unless you are in their custody (arrested) and they are asking questions that if answered could result in self-incrimination. A general question like "What happened?" is an appropriate question, because the officer has to find out the reason for the call and if there is anyone who might need medical attention in addition to other lifesaving information. It should be noted, whether a police officer advises you of your rights or not, everything you say can be used against you.

I have had the opportunity to interview and interrogate people of various races, ethnicities, socio-economic backgrounds, levels of education, age, gender and sexual orientation but many of them refused to use their right to remain silent. Ladies and gentlemen, you cannot *trick* the investigator! These folks are generally the more knowledgeable officers in the department. They are the ones with all the training to get you to tell on yourself. You can't beat them! So, stop trying.

Once you have been arrested, you will have some sort of court hearing. Your location's court structure will determine if the court appearance will be in Magistrate court, District Court, State Court, etc. Some jurisdictions call the initial court proceeding first appearance, and some may call it a bond hearing. Regardless of what it is called, this is not the appearance that establishes whether you are guilty or innocent. The first appearance is to determine whether a bond is appropriate and the amount of that bond. The judge will then set a bond, if the charges allow it. At this time you can request a preliminary hearing. If the police arrested you on a warrant a judge thought there was enough probable cause to arrest you. So, a preliminary hearing would be a waste of time, but it is your *right* to have one. During the preliminary hearing, the judge will hear testimony from the arresting officer to determine if there is probable cause for the arrest. If there is probable cause, the case will be *bound over* (transferred) to the court that would hear that particular charge. If the charge is a misdemeanor, the case will be heard in State Court. If the charge is a felony, the case will be heard in Superior Court.

If you can afford an attorney, it is best that you contact one as soon as you get arrested. If you cannot afford an attorney, one will be appointed to you. It is my opinion that the court appointed attorneys are very busy and have astronomical caseloads—this means that you are probably not their priority. Their job is to dispose of cases, by any means necessary. So, if you aren't guilty and are hoping to prove that point, you have to take a very active role in your defense. Do not simply sit back and depend on the court-appointed attorney to clear your name on their own. The most popular means of disposing of cases is the plea bargain. My spouse asked me one day "What is up with all of this plea-bargaining?" I told her it is a means to dispose of cases, without the cost of having a trial. Jury duty is not the top thing to do on most people's bucket list. It takes lots of jurors to choose from when planning a trial. If the court can avoid this they will. During the plea bargain, the accused person is offered a deal. The specifics of the deal depend on what the charge or charges were. In most cases, plea bargains involve lengthy probation sentences instead of jail time. While on probation you are not in jail, but you agree to forfeit or give up certain rights, such as your right to be secure from unreasonable search and seizure.

The commission of a felony takes on a different process. The process differs by the addition of the presentation to the Grand Jury. In Georgia, the county prosecutor is responsible for presenting felony cases to the grand jury, in each county. The grand jury is made up of 16 to 26 people, which includes three alternates. The grand jury hears cases involving felony charges. Their job is to determine if there is probable cause to justify the charge(s). The jurors listen to the testimony of investigators, police officers, witnesses, and victims of incidents, and they compare the alleged criminal acts and evidence collected to the elements of the crime the person was charged with. Then they determine if it is probable that a reasonable person would believe a crime was being committed—not necessarily that the crime was actually committed, but that a reasonable person on scene at the time of the crime believed a crime was being committed. If the grand jury believed there was probable cause that the accused committed the criminal act it results in a "True Bill." The paperwork that explains that the Grand Jury found probable cause is called the "Indictment."

Because of recent events involving grand juries, I think it should be noted when a grand jury is convened to hear a case against a police officer they may be instructed that probable cause is different for police officers. It changes from what a reasonable person would do to what a reasonable police officer would do. This comes from the United States Supreme Court case Graham v. Connor which established the standard of objective reasonableness. Because of the training and experience of police officers, the actions they take would not be the same as a regular citizen. Police officers are held to a different standard, when it comes to probable cause. In most cases an officer has only a spilt second to make life or death decisions. An average citizen may not see those situations the same as an officer would at the time of the incident. Hindsight is not afforded to an officer prior to making such decisions.

Personal Anecdote: I will offer you an example: *I see things that the average citizen may not see. My actions are actions that I would take because of my knowledge, training, and experiences. As I was traveling through a neighborhood I noticed a person dressed in all black walk across the street and into a driveway. The person, who was wearing a hooded sweat jacket ducked behind a car. As I saw them, I slowed down a little and observed from the rear view mirror to see if the person may have just dropped something, but I didn't believe this was the case. I observed the person run back across the street from the direction they came from. I called the police and told them what I saw and then knocked on the door to* alert the homeowner. They inspected their Jeep Cherokee, which had damage to the passenger side door lock. Based on my knowledge, training and experience, this damage was consistent in vehicle thefts. This scenario may have seemed perfectly normal to the average citizen. It is rare that an average citizen could see what a police officer sees, unless they've had previous law enforcement knowledge, training, and experience or in some past life they were a car thief.

Conviction

Conviction of a crime is not the end of the world. We learn from our mistakes and move on. However, a conviction could temporarily take away some of your constitutional rights, prevent you from earning a livable wage, or prolong the pursuit of higher education. A misdemeanor crime can result in a fine, jail time of one year or less, probation, or any combination of the three. A felony conviction can result in a fine, jail time of one year or more in prison, probation or any combination of the three.

A felony conviction automatically revokes (takes away) your right to vote; however, after the completion of your sentence, including any fines that apply to your sentence, your right to vote may be restored (depending on the state). *However, you will need to register again!* Even though your right to vote has been restored, your right to serve as a juror or run for political office may not be automatically restored. You may have to complete a restoration of rights application to restore these rights. You may be required to wait after the completion of your sentence and be crime free for some specified amount of time. Voting and serving on juries are important. Even if you have made a little mistake, you should feel obligated to get out of jail and register to vote. Although it is your right, it is also your responsibility. Again your failure to vote is a vote for the other team.

Being convicted of a felony also revokes (takes away) your right to bear arms (be in possession of a gun). If you have been convicted of a felony and are stopped while in possession of a firearm, you will be arrested. Having a weapon in your home is a problem, especially, if you are on probation or parole. By giving up your right against unreasonable search and seizure a parole or probation officer has the authority to enter your home, unannounced, at any time, to conduct a search. Even if your spouse has a weapon in the home, it could violate your probation or parole.

The right to bear arms in Georgia can only be restored after waiting five years after the completion of your sentence. During those five years you must be crime free. You will need letters of reference and must complete a personal interview. The chance to have your right to bear arms returned to you says everyone makes mistakes; however, it is what you do after you make that mistake that says what kind of person you are.

Probation

Do not be fooled, probation is not about you, the offender, but more about the cost to house offenders. Jail cells cost money to the states, counties, and cities that are responsible for running them. As crime goes up, citizens make their pleas to government officials to do something about it, but the revolving door at the local jail doesn't stop turning. Police chiefs and mayors, alike, are under fire for crime rates every day. They try to keep those numbers as low as possible, so they can tell you, after you and your neighbors' homes have been broken into, "According to the crime statistics, we are doing an outstanding job on crime." The problem is that the offenders were probably recently released from jail. To help with the growing costs of incarceration of the criminal element, in comes the private sector to rescue our beloved governments. Hence, the creation of private probation companies and prisons. Probation seems to have gotten out of control, for those who can't pay anyway. The issue with probation is, when someone is sentenced to probation, they have to pay a service fee. The private probation company that takes the case determines the fees to be paid. Now, being on probation allows you to work and continue to earn a living. In some cases, if you become unable to pay the service fee for any reason you may then be arrested and carted off to jail. The private probation company then becomes a bill collector with the power to obtain a criminal arrest warrant, one thing the ordinary bill collector doesn't have. Sometimes people might avoid a bill collector's calls and letters or the repo man's constant attempts to take their vehicle. Well, you can't avoid the probation man because he is not going to call and chase you around. He is simply going to go to court and request an arrest warrant for you. Now everywhere you go there is the potential that you will be arrested and taken to jail to serve time for a probation service fee that you couldn't afford in the first place.

My suggestion is know the law so that you don't break it. Think about this: If every jurisdiction gave up their financial responsibility of the prisons, jails, and probation they would save a lot of money. Wow, they could spend that savings on lowering taxes or on much needed infrastructure repair or even transportation. Let's do it, right? Wrong! Private industry and private companies come with high priced lobbyists that pay our good government officials perks, give them gifts, promise jobs for family members and good friends, nest eggs for after their public service careers, and on and on and on. These people have true influence on the laws of the land. Private run jails and probations, with no or limited government oversight, is a slippery slope that can only go bad. Imagine all state services being performed with probation, parole, and prison workers. Sounds good until you think about the thousands of people who would be out of work. You see, these companies can require these offenders to do whatever job they tell them to do to "work off" their time or fines. I did not say modern day "S" word here, but if you are thinking it, you are on the right track. Ladies and gentlemen, we have to educate ourselves about what is going on. Get out of the fog!

Probation is a means to avoid jail time, but it can be an awful alternative. Just obey the law and don't worry about probation. The public defender is there to dispose of your case. If you can afford an attorney, get one. Usually, the attorneys that handle misdemeanor cases are generally new or inexperienced attorneys. A seasoned, private attorney can assist in bringing your case to a reasonable close. Make sure your attorney is in good standing with the Bar Association in your state. You can find this online (example State Bar of Georgia: gabar.org).

Personal Anecdote: *I once was involved in a criminal case in which a suspect was facing several felony charges and was now in front of a judge for a preliminary hearing to determine if there was sufficient probable cause to go forward. The public defender was as prepared as they normally are, but the prosecutor did absolutely no preparation. There were no questions asked of me, prior to the case being heard. They were unclear on when to object or even what questions to ask. The victim was livid that the felony charges were reduced to one meaningless misdemeanor all because of the inexperience of the prosecutor. It was shameful because throughout the case the judge and the defense attorney were looking at the prosecutor as if they were incompetent in performing their duties.*

Looking at the justice system from the inside, I believe that one's socioeconomic status and education level can be a contributing factor for repeated interactions with law enforcement.

Also, the unwillingness or inability to learn how the criminal justice system works might be an additional contributing factor for repeated interactions with some aspects of the system.

Some police officers, at times, tend to help people who are either like themselves, remind them of someone they know, or just people who they generally like. So, when a police officer uses his or her discretion they may decide to help those people who look like them, those who are generally nice, or those who remind them of people they are familiar with. Discretion is when an officer has a choice in what actions they will take or if they take any action. Officers can decide, in some cases, whether to arrest, not arrest, write a ticket, not write a ticket, or write a warning; however, this discretion is not always available. Some laws and department policies specifically require that an arrest be made. So, this goes back to what I said about being calm and being "the bigger person" when encountering a police officer. In many cases, whether you realize it or not, your reaction to the officer may set the stage for what will occur next.

11
Children

Rule #11*: The Juvenile Justice System is very different. Understanding the goals and how it works can help parents prevent negative interactions with their children and law enforcement officers.*

The juvenile justice system is a bit difficult for some to swallow, especially victims. In order to understand it you have to first know the goal of the juvenile justice system. Their purpose is to protect the citizens and hold the offenders accountable, but they also attempt to rehabilitate those offenders to become responsible adult citizens. The juvenile justice system and how it operates tends to be the subject of debate between victims and parents of offenders. Of course victims would like to see their offenders locked up indefinitely but that is rarely the case. Parents of offenders rarely believe their child could be guilty of any crime and if they do believe their kid is capable of committing a crime their child should be given a second, third, fourth, or more opportunities to get it together. The justice system offers a combination of both with a lofty goal of rehabilitating the juvenile offender. The thought is to hold them accountable but also provide services to assist them with whatever underlying causes that may have led the juvenile to commit criminal or delinquent acts. Juvenile offenders are referred to as delinquents rather than criminals. Generally, when they are placed in handcuffs the act is considered a detainment rather than being called an arrest. The words delinquent and detainment may appear to be a little less serious and may prevent the child from feeling like their world has come to an end during the process, thus allowing them and their parents to completely buy into the methods involved in the rehabilitation process.

In Georgia, youth who are detained for felony or misdemeanor crimes are assessed to determine if they will be detained until a probable cause hearing or if they will be released to their parents. This procedure uses a point system in which each offense is assigned a certain number of points. The number of open cases or accumulated points determines if the detained juvenile will be held until an adjudication hearing (trial) or released to their parents. The juvenile procedure gets under the skin of law enforcement officers who work hard to capture juvenile offenders and complete the necessary paperwork to complete the process just to have the child released to their parents. In some cases the same officer who detained the offender may have to transport the offender home to their parent. The way the system operates sometimes discourages officers from dealing with juveniles while on patrol. Generally, if a crime is reported the officers will relentlessly follow up to locate offenders. But self-initiated activity is sometimes limited to adults because of the additional paperwork and juvenile procedures.

Adult criminals take advantage of the leniency of the Juvenile Justice System by recruiting children to commit crimes. The probability of a juvenile getting probation and the adult getting no punishment for a crime is 99.9 percent. This is why if you turn on the news you see juvenile offenders committing robberies, burglaries, shoplifting, motor vehicle thefts, drug offenses and on and on and on. Adults sell these kids the hope of having nice clothes, shoes, and money in their pockets. To them, crime pays. When I was a kid you would see kids throwing papers, mowing grass, running errands and cleaning to make money. These days delinquent children rob, steal, and burglarize to make money. Times have changed and you can pretty much point the finger at a number of causes like young parents, the economy, which requires parents to have two or more jobs and the inability of parents to effectively parent due to having a "friend mentality". Why are there so many children out and about, walking the streets in the early morning hours, during school time, or any other time? It could be a number of reasons but the ability of parents to effectively monitor their children and provide adequate consequences for breaking rules is a start. Juvenile reform is centered around parental involvement. The government is decreasing their responsibility in raising children. Time and time again children are released to parents to address the discipline problems and criminal activity children are involved in. Juvenile court and detention facilities are cutting costs; which means, parents have to take more responsibility in the rehabilitation of their children.

Parental involvement is the key to making children responsible for their actions. Involvement in school is a start. Effective parenting has to begin when children are very young. I have seen small toddlers cursing their parents and the parents just laugh believing they have no idea what they are saying. Children are very smart and receptive of what goes on around them. When the behavior is acceptable at a young age they grow up and believe the behavior is still acceptable. So, a 2 year old child cursing an adult is funny but at 8 the parent wants to try to correct the behavior. Sorry it is too late at that time. The corrections have to come when the behavior is first observed. It takes a village to raise children, but the village is becoming increasingly smaller. Parents alone cannot accomplish this task successfully. Trusted family members should also be involved with correcting unacceptable behavior when children are young. A family member who allows unacceptable behavior in their presence is no different than a parent who allows that behavior. Children are like sponges. They retain everything that is modeled for them which makes it that much more important for adults to model acceptable behavior when in the presence of children. Behaviors such as consuming alcohol, sex, using narcotics including smoking marijuana, cursing people, responding to situations with anger, fighting, robbing people, stealing from people, purchasing stolen goods, cheating, etc. are unacceptable and should not be modeled and spoken of in the presence of children. The influence sometimes creates a belief in children that if the behavior is acceptable for an adult it is acceptable for them. While on patrol I encountered a juvenile who was skipping school. I picked the juvenile up to transport him back to school. As I was speaking with the juvenile I smelled the odor of fresh marijuana. I conducted a pat down of the juvenile for weapons (department policy) before I placed him inside my patrol vehicle. I did not locate any weapons and transported the juvenile to school. Upon arrival I informed the principal that I smelled fresh marijuana on the juvenile. The principal conducted a search of the student's bag and located a plastic bag containing ten smaller plastic bags that contained what appeared to be marijuana. I asked the student if his parents knew he smoked marijuana and I was surprised to hear him say his mother did know. I asked the mother if she knew her child was smoking marijuana and she said she did know but told him not to bring it to school. WHAT??? Based on what she said we cited the mother for contributing to the delinquency of a minor and contacted the Department of Family and Child Services. It is not acceptable for parents to allow their **children** to be involved in clearly illegal activities. A parent cannot wait until a child is in middle school to begin disciplining the child for unacceptable behavior it has to begin in the early ages.

    Most of the juvenile delinquents that I have come in contact with have had issues in school. Their grades are often failing and attendance is also poor or non-existent. A parent who goes to work and only looks at a report card every six or so weeks is not an effective parent these days. The parent has to make contact with teachers and get involved in the education of their children before issues arise. Yes, it is difficult because parents also want to enjoy life, but they have to take responsibility and get involved in their children's life, ALL OF IT. If you are not involved at your child's school now, you may be forced to get involved with them in the justice system. So, I ask why not get involved in the education of your child early to prevent you from becoming involved in the justice system later? Be an observant parent. If your child comes home with clothing that *you* didn't buy, they had to have gotten the items somewhere. Ask questions and don't settle for BS answers. Follow up. You have to be a detective to have kids these days. If they have items you didn't buy, the child doesn't need them. If your child asks to spend the night with someone, go and meet the other child's parent, get a phone number for them, and make sure they are responsible enough to keep your child. If their child is hanging out all night, your child should not spend the night there. If little Johnnie has a cell phone you didn't buy, whether it is active or not, you have to have a conversation with him. Ask where he got the phone. Ask if he is robbing or stealing. If a child buys an I-phone for a few dollars or traded some candy for it, trust it is probably stolen. Being in possession of a stolen phone is no different than stealing one in the eyes of the law. If you don't ask your children these tough questions some cop will have to. I would rather it be me talking to my children than a cop. Be involved. Be involved. Be involved, so the police don't have to!

Technology

Our children are our future. We shelter them, love them and care for them. As responsible adults we attempt to provide children with the guidance they will need to be productive citizens in this society. In some instances, children find themselves navigating through life without knowing the consequences of their actions and how those actions can impact their adult lives.

Technology has consumed our children's lives. They live, work and play on their phones. A common mantra among teachers is "please disconnect". Children are constantly on their phones whether they are listening to the latest tunes or connecting with a friend in the adjacent classroom. The use of cellphones have changed the way children interact with each other socially. Before the cellphone, messages were communicated verbally and with context, but now messages are communicated via social media and text messages. The context of these text messages and social media posts are not always conveyed. There are no facial expressions to go along with the message, no voice inflection that might allow the message receiver to determine exactly how the message was supposed to be received. Another issue text messages and social media posts present is the immediacy of messages. A child is able to express an opinion immediately without thought of how the message will be received or the consequences of sending that message. Social media and text messages have made it much easier for children to immediately confront each other about unverified information. Text messages and social media posts become a police issue when those posts and texts instigate fights where children suffer injuries. Children are too quick to fight about what someone said about them. Our children have to learn conflict resolution; but to do this, they have to actually speak and be able to explain their feelings clearly and calmly. My mother repeatedly told me, "It is not what you say but how you say it." She was right, but I would like to take that a step further and say it is also how the message is interpreted and received. It is my responsibility to do everything I can, such as using my tone, facial expressions, hand gestures, examples to ensure the message I am sending is the message that is being received. This is the definition of communication and why communicating via text and social media posts is so difficult.

Although it is difficult for children to understand, they must realize they cannot control what other people say about them. The example I use when addressing this issue with children is, if I were to walk into a room filled with people and as I walked through the room everyone was saying something negative about me would I attempt to fight everyone or confidently exit the room? Generally, after a few minutes of thought, the child comes to the conclusion that the best thing to do is to leave. Next, I ask them "You would just walk away?" They usually respond ,"Yes, I can't fight them all." Generally at that moment they get it, they can't fight everyone who says negative things about them. I follow up by telling them "Your issue is not new. Throughout life there will always be someone who will not agree with you, who will not like you or who will not like things about you." Children want to be liked, accepted and well received. They find it difficult to understand and accept when they aren't. As adults we have to reinforce the positive attributes children have and insure they are bombarded with positive images that will promote positive growth in them.

Social media posts and text messaging have also facilitated an increase in bullying. According to the website *Stopbullying.gov* bullying is unwanted aggressive behavior that involves a real or perceived power imbalance. Acts that can be considered bullying include: making threats, spreading rumors, attacking someone physically or verbally, and excluding someone from a group on purpose. Children bully each other for a number of reasons. A girl who is receiving attention from a boy who shows other girls attention may be a victim of bullying. Boys who are reluctant to join a particular group in a school might be a victim of bullying. A child who excels in areas such as choir, art and orchestra may be bullied because those activities may not be considered "boy" activities. Children who identify as LGBTQ, children who are considered weak or unable to defend themselves, children who have outwardly different appearances or speak differently and children who have low self-esteem or are unpopular could all be victims of bullying. Conversely, children who are more likely to be bullies are those who are concerned with their popularity, those who are aggressive in their actions, children who have difficulty following rules, children who view violence in a positive manner and children who have issues at home.

There are laws that prohibit bullying in almost every state. These laws are generally used to craft bullying policies for state and local educational bodies to deter, track and address incidents of bullying. Threats of violence, whether verbal or via social media, is hurtful to children and unlawful. This immediate, unverified information that is shared through text messages and social media posts have instigated fights and caused children to lose their self-worth. Children are more likely to take an "I don't care" attitude after they believe their "friends" have spoken negatively about them on social media. Children have to understand people will talk about them but not to allow that to get them down and upset to the point they are willing to solve the issue with violence.

Technology and the use of cellphones has allowed children to be "exposed" sexually. I learned from speaking to a high school student that girls are susceptible to being "exposed" when they agree to have sex with some boys. The games boys play to encourage girls to have sex with them is no different than in the past but the consequences are long lasting, more hurtful and can even be deadly. Our girls are having sex ignorant to the long term impacts such as diseases, pregnancy, negative social reputation and failing grades. Social media posts that denigrate a child can be detrimental to their future. Parents have to ensure their children know the consequences of their actions. Being a friend to your child in not the way to do this. You have to have open lines of communication with not only your child, but your child's teachers and school administrators to have a clear and complete picture of your child. If you are waiting on the teacher to contact you about problems you have waited too late!

Children need their father's more than ever in these times! Girls need their father's to love them and teach them the games that boys play. Boys tell girls what they believe they want or need to hear to get their mission accomplished. This needs to be pounded into the heads of young girls. Girls have to be taught it is not acceptable for boys to disrespect her, whether he is "playing" or not. Same gender relationships are no different, regardless of who a girl is dating there is no excuse for allowing that person to be disrespectful. Girls have to be taught they should not settle for less than the best, just to say they are "with" someone. Some mothers may need to realize this as well. It is ok to wait for our partner to show us their best on a consistent basis and not just enough to accomplish the goal of sex. Boys are also in need of good, responsible fathers. Young boys need a father to teach them how to become responsible men, how to be a caregiver, supportive of their families and to love unconditionally. They need a man to teach them to wear their pants on their hips rather than under their behinds. They need fathers to teach them how to tie a necktie for graduation. Our children are starving for love and acceptance of their fathers. I could not imagine growing up without my father. I see some young girls and know they are missing out on the love of a "good" father. No "man" is perfect, but my father came awfully close in my eyes! Our girls are more susceptible to being tricked into believing and doing things they would not do with the guidance of a father. Mother's do an awesome job at standing in but all children need their fathers as well. It pains me to hear my colleagues complain about child support. Children need more than a few dollars every month. They need to know they are loved and understood by their fathers. They need hugs and to be reassured they are important. They need to know they can be successful and that they too, can be great. My father always reassured me of these things. Non- traditional families that are composed of two same gender parents should surround their child with adult role models of the opposite sex to provide insight from a different perspective.

Technology has allowed people to be fooled into relationships, tricked into providing personal information and even nude photos. This online behavior is called "catfishing". It is accomplished when someone pretends to be someone else to obtain something from someone. Predators use this tactic to encourage communication with children. Children who publicly post their feelings of despair and needs of material things are susceptible to predators and human traffickers. A child wanting expensive clothes, jewelry and shoes can be an opening for these type people. Parents have to model to children that these things are not necessary to be successful. They have to ensure material things do not drive their children, especially if they are unwilling or unable to provide these things. Parenting today requires a lot more work than in the past. I can remember having a great fear of defying or even embarrassing my parents. Some children have no fear of anything, especially their parents. The lessons that children learn from their mistakes are much greater today. They need constant guidance and supervision. Yes, you will upset them and they won't like you but in the end they will thank you! There is no manual and I don't believe anyone said it would be easy. If you thought it would be I'm sorry you were wrong. I have spoken to more than a few children who said, "I wish my parent cared enough to listen to me." They want you to listen without interruption. Don't tell them "I know what you are going through" because they believe their problems are unique. Hear them out and then ask them is it ok to give them a bit of advice. This has worked for a police officer that has no idea about what they are going through. In most cases they are willing to receive the message, not because I am so wise, but because I listened **completely and without judgement**.

Unwanted touching is another issue that children endure. Both boys and girls have endured unwanted touching by other children. This touching comes from both same and opposite sex. Our children have to know what is appropriate and what is not. They have to have the self-confidence to say to their peers "please don't touch me like that." I see an uneasy look from children as their peers touch them on their buttocks, breasts, genitals and rub their shoulders without setting boundaries. Girls think when boys touch them inappropriately it is ok or they hesitate to set boundaries for fear of being ostracized by boys they like. Children have to know they are valuable without someone touching them inappropriately. They have to understand they don't have to give away their self-worth to be accepted.

Accidental shootings by children is a growing issue in this country. As more and more people feel the need to arm themselves, whether it is acknowledgement of their 2nd Amendment Right or to protect themselves and their homes from criminals, children have increasingly come into contact with firearms. Their curiosity and fascination with firearms have resulted in numerous senseless injuries and deaths as a result of accidental shootings by children. Regardless of an adult's reasoning for possessing a firearm there is a need to teach children about the dangers those firearms pose. Small children are enamored with the movement of the trigger. This is the one part of a firearm they are able to manipulate easily. There is also the mystery of the dark barrel. The combination of manipulating the trigger and looking into the dark barrel results in a child shooting themselves in the face or chest. This can be avoided by simply teaching them, in advance, of the dangers firearms pose. I am not implying children need to learn to shoot but rather the trigger can cause a bullet to come out of the barrel which can cause them to harm themselves or someone else. My book *Brownie Bear Teaches Gun Safety* is a great resource for parents to use in teaching their children about the dangers of firearms.

12 CREATING CHANGE

Rule #12: *There are many things we can do to improve negative interactions with law enforcement but the first is to understand law enforcement, the rules they operate by and how those rules are created. The second is to become involved in the rule making process.*

Politics is a funny thing, the negativity, unknowns, untruths and lack of knowledge about the issues at stake can sometimes discourage participation in our "Democracy." It is often difficult to muddle through all of the slush, the proposed plans and how they will impact you personally but that is the point. People get so frustrated in their quest to decipher the legal jargon and break down the issues into digestible bites that we can understand and the difficulty in understanding creates a feeling of helplessness and apathy which discourages participation. We have to be more aware of the process and get involved. There is no class to take. We have to open a book and read. Read about the Electoral College and how it works. Read about how elections can impact you personally on both a local and national level. We have to stop depending on the news to provide us with the answers. If this past election has taught us nothing else it has provided us with clear examples that the news can be spun to benefit whoever is spinning it. It can be totally made up or presented to be something it is not. There will never be a political candidate who will say everything you want or believe 100% what you believe. Politicians are trained to say what the people want to hear. They make promises they know they cannot deliver on or are misguided to believe they can deliver on things they are unable to deliver on. You cannot be bamboozled into believing that any politician can deliver on EVERYTHING they promise. You have to research their history and know what they have stood for in the past. People's fundamental beliefs do not change. A saying I learned and truly believe is, "When people show you who they are, believe them." Not sure who came up with that one but they definitely hit the nail on the head. I can't help but remember a conversation with a friend who was adamant about not voting for Hillary Clinton because he was for Bernie Sanders. I told him, "Unfortunately, Bernie did not get the nomination, so you do understand not voting for the candidate who did get the nomination may as well be a vote for the opposition?" Hillary had flaws for sure just as Bernie had, but she was the party nominee and not voting for her was the same as voting for the opposition. He, like many others for whatever reason, decided not to cast a vote in the Presidential Election. This was a huge mistake.

    Politics and voting has an impact on every aspect of our lives. Highly publicized incidents involving deadly police citizen encounters can be traced back to politics and voting. I was so glad to see *peaceful* protests for all of the people who were killed during those deadly encounters. My heart goes out to those parents who lost children and those children who lost parents. But what happens when the protesting is over and everyone has gotten back to their daily routines? In some cases, nothing. The politicians get back to leading their respective governments, police departments get back to protecting and serving, victims try to adjust to a new normal, but nothing constructive really happens. Unfortunately these incidents like a lot of incidents are viewed on a personal level (how does this impact ME right now). The laws that are currently written must be understood and analyzed on a micro and macro level, specifically how they impact someone personally and how they impact the larger population. Those laws that are ineffective should be modified to address issues that cause them to be ineffective.

Voter registration impacts the diversity of jury pools. You cannot be selected as a potential juror if you are not registered to vote. Jury duty is an unpopular civic duty for a number of reasons including fear of retaliation and loss of wages and time at work. As more and more people attempt to get out of jury duty local juries miss out on diverse thinking people to decide the fate of people accused of criminal activity. Jury duty is an important aspect of the criminal justice system and citizen participation is necessary to ensure the criminal justice system works. It is critical for our jury pools to be diverse and include people who have different life experiences, thoughts and beliefs. It is important for those people to be able to debate the elements involved in both criminal and civil cases with objectivity. How can we positively impact the criminal justice system when we are unwilling to take part in those processes that require our representation?

Voting also impacts the laws related to the police such as police use of force and use of deadly force. Typically laws are pretty clear. Either you did it or you didn't do it and the evidence either supports the crime was committed or it doesn't. With police officers it's a bit different. The activity was done but the jury has to decide if the act was reasonable. To add further confusion the reasonableness is based on a reasonable officer not a reasonable civilian. The reasonableness requirement takes into account the specialized training an officer receives and the necessity to make a split second life or death decision. Throughout my time in the field training program I often heard beat officers saying "I would rather be judged by 12 than carried by 6." They meant they would accept their chances with a jury rather than being killed. It all goes back to the goal of making it home each day. The question then becomes would a reasonable officer do the same thing given the same situation. It is very difficult for me as an officer to say what I would do in a situation without being in that position because I am unaware of all of the dynamics involved.

To impact real change protests must be coupled with action such as registering to vote, finding out where your polling place is, researching potential politicians/proposed legislation and voting at every election. Making change involves attending board meetings, introducing yourself to representatives and discussing plans for your community. I had to take a look at my own lack of community involvement. I have begun an open line of communication with my local county commissioner to improve certain aspects within my community. Voting is only one step in being involved in the political process, albeit a very big step. We have to be knowledgeable of when an election is occurring and who or what is on the ballot. I encourage researching ballot issues and candidates to determine if the issues will have a positive impact on you and your community and to determine candidates philosophies and voting histories. The most irresponsible thing someone could do is to vote for someone simply because they are running as a Democrat or Republican or because they are black or white or male or female. We should be voting for candidates because they will represent what we believe in and vote for polices that reflect where we want our communities to go. When those politicians fail to represent the wishes of the constituents we must remove them. To do that we must remain informed about our political representative's activities.

I find it simply astonishing that during the 2008 and 2012 presidential elections there were lines out the doors and wrapped around buildings from the early voting period until election day but during the more important local school board, mayor, council person, state representative, and congressional elections there are only small numbers of voters casting ballots. Ladies and gentlemen, these are the elections that determine local issues—people that make the laws where we live. They vote to raise taxes or not on gas, groceries and other necessities. They pass laws that determine who can carry firearms and where they carry them. They make laws that determine what your children learn in school. They determine how many times your garbage will be collected and how much you will pay for water. Presidential elections are important but local elections are just as important if not more important. What I am saying is your vote matters. *Vote at every opportunity!* A lot of people died for *everyone* in this country to have this right and yet we do not take responsibility to vote and get involved. I know people who, to this day, still do not vote because they believe their vote doesn't count. I don't know how to express this any clearer—the failure to vote is the same as a vote for the opposition.

I was speaking with a young man about politics and I was taken aback by his comments. He expressed his disdain for the current President and his political views. As we were concluding our conversation I told him to make sure when he turns 18 that he votes. He turned and stated he won't be voting because his vote doesn't count. I informed him that many people lost their lives so that we could have the "Right" to vote. He stated he understood and respected those people. I immediately corrected him and stated, "If you say you can't vote because your vote doesn't count then you are not respecting those people who sacrificed their lives for you to vote. It is not only a Right to vote but a Responsibility to vote." I informed him there were many people who felt the way he did and they failed to vote in the last Presidential election which is a contributing factor to the election of the current President.
I went on to tell him the only way to change the politics is to get involved and encourage everyone he knows to get involved.

I met a parent who complained about a local school. She complained about the number of behavioral distractions her son told her about in his 7th grade class. She was unhappy with the response from administrators when she complained to them. She was disappointed that teachers were not being compensated more for their efforts. I asked her who was her school board representative but she did not know. I asked her if she voted and she said she did not. How can we expect our voices to be heard if we are unaware and we do not vote.

X, Georgia

I would like to use this example to bring home the point of felony convictions, voting, and lack of representation. Let's take a make believe city called X, Georgia. The city representatives identify themselves as follows: the Mayor, who is elected by the people of the city is white, the Police Chief, who is appointed by the Mayor is white, the District Attorney, who is elected by the people is white, and the Superior Court Judge who is elected by the people is white.

The population in city X is 1,000 people. The census (which is important to complete) says of the 1,000 people, 500 are voting age adults. Of those 500 working age adults, 200 identify themselves as black, 150 as Hispanic, 100 as white and 50 as Asian.

Of the 200 adults that identify themselves as black 50 percent of these adults have been convicted of felonies, which brings the number of *eligible voters* to 100. In this state people convicted of a felony cannot vote.

Of the 100 eligible black voters 60 percent either believe their vote doesn't count, are disinterested in the candidates, or they are unwilling to go vote, which brings the number of eligible participating voters to 40. Of the 40 eligible voters, 30 percent won't come out to vote if it is raining, which brings the number of eligible voters to 12.

Of the 150 people who identified themselves as Hispanic, 50 percent were convicted of felonies, which brings the number of eligible voters to 75, and another 80 percent are undocumented, which brings the number of eligible voters to 15. Of the 15 eligible voters 20 percent won't come out to vote in the rain, which brings the number of eligible voters to 12.

Of the 50 people who identify themselves as Asian, 2 percent are convicted felons, which brings the number of eligible voters to 49. Of the 49 eligible Asian voters, 10 percent are undocumented, which brings the number of eligible voters to 44. Of the 44 eligible voters, four percent won't come out to vote if it is raining, which brings the number of eligible voters to 42. Of the 42 eligible voters, 80 percent don't believe their vote will count, are disinterested in the candidates or are unwilling to go vote, which brings the number of voting people to 8.

Of the 100 people who identify as white, 50 percent are convicted felons, which brings the number of eligible voters to 50. Of the 50 eligible voters, 10 percent won't come out to vote in the rain, which brings the number of eligible voters to 45. Of the 45 eligible voters, 20 percent believe their vote won't count, are disinterested in the candidates, or are unwilling to go vote, bringing the number of eligible voters to 36.

In summary, there are 12 eligible black voters, 8 Asian voters, 12 Hispanic voters, and 36 white voters.

The numbers used in this example are arbitrary and do not come from any particular source. The example attempts to show how population does not necessarily equal representation. Representation is a result of people running for office and *voting*. If you, as an adult, regardless of your race or ethnicity are not spreading the word about how important voting is, you should be!

There is not a racial or prejudice issue in city X but there is a voter issue. Voting will not solve every problem, but we would hope it helps in increasing fair representation. If you are not a citizen of this country then you should take the necessary steps to become a citizen so that you can take part in the political process. This country is a true melting pot with every person having an opinion. I would like to think that voting gives your opinion a voice. Let's get involved and be the change we are seeking.

To make significant changes all members of society must become engaged in the political process. It is not enough to know the rules of engagement and simply sit on the sidelines and wait for someone else to make something happen. We have to be active in our communities and involved in making them better. We shouldn't have to move to be comfortable but rather take ownership of where we are, self included.

EPILOGUE

As I stated in the beginning, this book was a result of many friends and associates asking law enforcement related questions. Although it has Georgia all over it the concepts can be used in any state. I recommend you do some research about your local laws and ordinances. I truly believe that knowledge is power. In light of so many publicized incidents involving interactions with law enforcement, I felt compelled to put something on paper that might help people understand what they should expect from the police based on my own personal experiences. While in my personal car, outside of my uniform, I have had interactions with police officers. Some were positive and some were not so positive. I have interacted with officers who act professionally and I have interacted with officers who did not act professionally. The purpose here is not to make you believe that all police officers are bad people, nor is it to make you believe that all police officers are good people, just for you to know what can happen, what should happen, and what to do if you feel unsatisfied. I hope it was a pleasant read for you. Please pass it on to all of your family and friends.

Be safe!

ABOUT THE AUTHOR

B.L. Brown has been in the law enforcement field for over 15 years. She has served as a Special Operations Investigator, Community Oriented Policing Officer, Detective, Field Training Officer, Senior Instructor and Supervisor.

Ms. Brown has taught numerous subjects in the criminal justice field at local training academies. She has written several training manuals for law enforcement agencies including: criminal investigations, field training officer and new officer orientation.

Ms. Brown has a Bachelor Degree in Education from Henderson State University and a Master Degree in Public Administration from Troy University, where she was a Phi Alpha Alpha Honor Graduate.

Ms. Brown has served as an adjunct instructor and looks forward to more teaching opportunities.

Ms. Brown considers herself as a lifelong learner and whole heartedly believes in the quote "give a man a fish and he will eat for a day, teach a man to fish and he will eat for a lifetime". (Author Unknown)

By knowing the rules we can change the outcomes. In this criminal justice system, we have to know the rules, the players and understand how to engage. That is the only way to change the outcomes. I hope that you enjoyed the book—it is meant to be thought provoking and not in any way legal advice. I am not an attorney, so I am not qualified to offer legal advice. If you need such advice, please seek *qualified* legal counsel.

Resources

Brown, Paul G. (2003), Post-Traumatic Stress Disorder in Law Enforcement

Center for Constitutional Rights (2012, October 1). Daniels, et al. v. the City of New York. https://ccrjustice.org/home/what-we-do/our-cases/daniels-et-al-v-city-new-york

Center for Constitutional Rights (2017, June 9). Floyd, et al. v. City of New York, et al. https://ccrjustice.org/home/what-we-do/our-cases/floyd-et-al-v-city-new-york-et-al

Fisher-Stewart, Gayle (2007) Community Policing Explained: A Guide for Local Government

Georgia Department of Driver Services https://dds.georgia.gov/suspensions-and-revocations

Georgia Law Enforcement Handbook. (2012-1013). Thomson Reuters

Grossman, Dave (2006), Preface: Hunting Wolves. *Global Crime*, 7, no. 3-4, 291-298

Haines, Corey (2003), Police Stress and the Effects on the Family

McKee, Adam J. (2002) Broken Windows Theory

Moskos, Peter (2008) Cop In The Hood

National Institute of Justice, Race, Trust and Police Legitimacy (2013, January 1). Racial Profiling. https://www.nij.gov/topics/law-enforcement/legitimacy/pages/racial-profiling.aspx

National Institute of Justice (2016, November 29). Police Use of Force. https://nij.gov/topics/law-enforcement/officer-safety/use-of-force/Pages/welcome.aspx

New York Civil Liberties Union (2017, May 23). Stop and Frisk Facts. https://www.nyclu.org/en/stop-and-frisk-facts

Paynich, Rebecca L. (2009) The Impact of a College-Educated Police Force: A review of the literature

Peak, Kenneth J. (2006) Policing America

United States Constitution

www.ingramcontent.com/pod-product-compliance
Lightning Source LLC
Chambersburg PA
CBHW020744180526
45163CB00001B/348